Better Homes and Gardens®

PATCHWORK & QUILTING

BETTER HOMES AND GARDENS® BOOKS
Editorial Director: Don Dooley
Executive Editor: Gerald Knox
Art Director: Ernest Shelton
Assistant Art Director: Randall Yontz
Production and Copy Editor: David Kirchner
Craft Editor: Nancy Lindemeyer
Senior Associate Craft Editor: Ciba Vaughan
Associate Craft Editor: Marie B. Schulz
Graphic Designers: Sheryl Veenschoten,
Faith Berven, Harijs Priekulis

CONTENTS

Even if you've never patched before, you'll be able to create wonderful, useful things from our easy-to-follow how-to instructions. Learn by doing is the approach taken in this introduction to patchwork.

Patchwork—
A Practical and Creative Craft

Once you've mastered the basics of patchwork, you're ready to go on to any number of pieced projects. Here are some challenging patterns to tackle.

Pieced Patchwork—
A Kaleidoscope of Patterns

Traditional—
American Quilts and Quilting

America's patchwork quilts are a heritage to be proud of. Once you become involved in patchwork, you'll be able to appreciate the true meaning of this historic craft. And when you make one of these beautiful quilts, you'll be part of the tradition.

Appliqué
An Added Dimension

To expand your skills and your design sources, learn how to appliqué. In this section, there's basic how-to information on both machine and hand appliqué. Included are such imaginative projects as a quilted headboard, a fabulous contemporary butterfly quilt, and a charming quilted "window" wall hanging.

Patchwork Plus—
Novelty Projects

Once you've mastered patchwork, quilting, and appliqué, there are any number of intriguing ways to use these practical crafts. For example, you can combine them with other techniques to achieve exciting new results.

It is difficult for us today to imagine how valuable and important small scraps of fabric were to our pioneer forebears. In a time when little was discarded, frugal homemakers saved the best parts of worn clothing and household items and then artfully stitched them into beautiful, warm quilts. That's how the truly American craft of patchwork was born. If you'd like to try your hand at this heritage craft, our book will guide you, stitch by stitch, through a collection of interesting and useful projects for your home that will make patchwork come alive for you.

Patchwork—

A Practical and Creative Craft

Not all patchwork is complex and time consuming. There are some attractive patterns that even first-time patchworkers can create. This section is designed to introduce you to the basics of patchwork through some quick-and-easy projects that will turn you on without scaring you off. Instructions for items shown here are on pages 24 and 25.

Patchwork Basics

Patchwork can be a simple combination of squares, or maybe a complex arrangement of several geometric shapes. But no matter what the design, all patchwork projects involve the same procedures—drafting a pattern, collecting materials, cutting and piecing shapes together to form blocks, and then joining the blocks to create pieced fabric. Here's what you need to know to make patchwork fabric for quilt tops, curtains, pillows, place mats, or any other item you want to fabricate with dazzling design and color.

Choosing a design is not only the first step in any patchwork project, it may well be the most difficult. It's easy to fall in love with one of the traditional patchwork patterns and attack it with great enthusiasm. But without sufficient experience it's a disappointment when you discover the project you chose isn't within your range of skills, and you either abandon or lose interest in it. So start slowly. Choose a simple patchwork pattern first, and then work up to the more impressive designs. There are dozens of beautiful patchwork patterns worked with nothing more complicated than squares and slashed squares (triangles). Pick one of these and you won't have any trouble—even with your very first project.

Collecting Fabrics

Traditionally, patchwork quilt tops have been made of calico, 100-percent cotton broadcloth, cotton percale, gingham, chintz, corduroy—and even some fancier fabrics such as velvet, satin, or taffeta. When choosing fabric for patchwork, don't lose sight of its washability. If the finished project is better off washable, stay away from satins, felts, velvets, or any fabric that must be cleaned.

Evaluate a fabric's characteristics and learn to avoid those that are difficult to use in patchwork. For instance, burlap or loosely woven fabrics ravel too easily to be practical. Heavy fabrics such as denim, sailcloth, or canvas are difficult to sew. Polyester knits are very stretchy, and linen wrinkles too easily. So, your best bet is to stick to cotton or cotton blend fabrics.

Mixing fabrics and patterns is a matter of personal taste. Some fabrics are natural go-togethers; others are not. For instance it won't take you long to realize that gingham and satin is probably not the combination you want. Keep textures in mind, too. On the one hand, a quilt top might be more interesting if it displays both smooth and textured fabrics. On the other hand, you may determine that the effect you want calls for fabrics all of one texture—or without any noticeable texture.

Print fabrics are perfectly at home in the potpourri that is patchwork. If you want the print to register as a color, choose a very small-scale print. A large-scale print will come off looking more like a texture when used in a large patchwork piece—or as no print at all when cut in small sections.

Though patchwork is a good way to utilize good pieces of worn-out garments or scraps from sewing projects, it takes years to develop a really well-rounded scrap bag. And the design you choose might dictate a definite color scheme—one you can't achieve with leftovers. In that case, you'll have to buy new goods. For fabric bargains, check mill outlets, remnant counters, and discount shops. If fabric is new, make sure it's preshrunk and colorfast. And wash all fabrics and press thoroughly before starting to cut.

Marking Your Fabric

The process of marking fabric starts with making a template of each piece in your patchwork design. A template is a pattern that can be used over and over. You can buy ready-made plastic or metal templates at craft supply shops, or make your own using sandpaper or lightweight cardboard. (Sandpaper will not slip when placed on fabric, so cutting pieces is easier.) Plan to make several templates of each pattern piece because the edges fray with repeated use and can interfere with the precision of your measurements. Accuracy is the secret to successful patchwork.

To make a template, enlarge the pattern shown on a grid to its actual working size. Graph paper can make enlarging a pattern piece easier and more accurate. When you have the piece enlarged, cover cardboard or sandpaper with carbon paper, face down, and place your enlarged pattern over it. Trace over the pattern lines, remove the graph paper and carbon, and cut out the template using a sharp craft knife or scissors.

Before cutting, mark on each template how many pieces of each color and print fabric you'll need. This will speed the cutting process since you won't have to stop to check the master design.

Find the straight grain of the fabric by looking at the selvage, or, on pieces with no selvage, by pulling a thread. Place the pattern piece template on the straight grain of the fabric. For square or rectangular pieces, all edges should be on the lengthwise or crosswise grain; diamond-shaped pieces should be cut with two edges on the straight grain. Right angle triangles should have two sides on the straight grain. All other shapes should have the straight grain running through the center of the piece.

If your patchwork is to be pieced, lay the fabric out so the wrong side is up. If it is to be appliquéd, have the right side of the fabric up so you can see just where the hems of the pieces are to be turned under for stitching. Place your template on the fabric and trace with a soft pencil.

Seam allowances are generally not given on patchwork patterns, so you'll have to add ¼ inch to all edges when cutting. Always remember that the pencil

line represents the line for sewing—not cutting. Study the top drawing on this page and note the solid tracing lines and the dotted cutting lines.

If you lay out your pattern pieces ½ inch apart, you can cut down the middle of the space between squares, creating a ¼-inch seam allowance and wasting almost no fabric. Add seam allowances to your template if you like. It's more work at the outset, but it may save you time if you're going to be cutting great quantities of squares.

Cutting Pattern Pieces

Make sure your scissors are really sharp. And always begin by laying the fabric out on a cutting board or a large flat surface.

To make the best use of your fabric, cut any border strips first. If your project pattern calls for long, continuous strips, cut them out of the full fabric lengths, then go on to cut the small pieces. Don't forget the ¼-inch seam allowance on border strips as well as pattern pieces.

Cut each piece individually, one at a time, to prevent the bottom layers of fabric from slipping. The only exception would be in the case of completely non-slip fabric. Then carefully pin two layers together to trim your cutting time in half.

Sort pieces according to color and shape as you cut your fabrics. One way to keep pieces in order is to string them together as shown in the bottom drawing on this page. Tie a knot in the end of a single thread and pull the needle through the center of each block. After stringing all the identical blocks onto the thread, remove the needle. Do this for each different group of size, shape, and color. Then as you need the blocks, simply slip them off the thread one at a time.

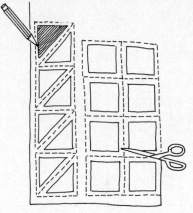

Marking and cutting fabric.

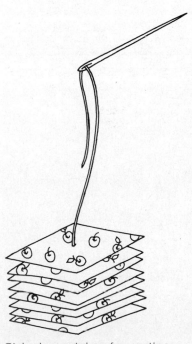

Stringing patches for sorting

continued

Patchwork Basics *(continued)*

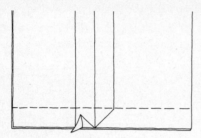

Trimming a seam

Pressing seams open

Piecing Your Fabric

"Piecing" patchwork fabric means sewing all the small pieces together to form blocks. This doesn't necessarily take a lot of experience and talent. What it takes is accuracy and patience.

Join patchwork pieces by hand or machine sewing. Purists among quilters might frown on machine "piecing," but few people today have the leisure time to hand stitch hundreds of pieces together to form a quilt.

However, there are some things to consider in deciding whether to hand sew or machine sew the pieces together. If the pattern pieces are very small, you may find they're difficult to handle on the sewing machine. The close stitches made by the machine may also make it difficult to hand quilt over them. You might consider a combination of the two methods. Hand stitch the pieces to form the blocks, then machine stitch the blocks together for added strength on long seams.

Hold the pattern pieces firmly in place with right sides together as you piece. There's no need to pin or baste short piecing seams, however the longer seams should be pinned to make sure all pieces line up properly and don't shift in the sewing. To hand sew, use tiny running stitches, if machine piecing, use medium length stitches. If your sewing machine has a lock stitch, you may find it helpful to use it. That way you can clip the threads at either end of the seam without having the seam open up. Without a lock stitch, you should fasten both ends of the seam by tacking with a back-and-forth stitch.

Seams should be fastened at either end when hand sewing, too. Do this by making several back-stitches.

If you've traced your pattern pieces on the wrong side of the fabric, without a seam allowance, you will have a pencil line to guide you in sewing a straight seam.

Don't stretch seams when sewing two bias edges together. Pull the thread taut to prevent stretching. It's a good idea to finger press the seams open as you go, making sure each seam is open before crossing with another seam. Trim out the excess fabric where seams cross in order to reduce bulk. See the top diagram on this page.

Piece one entire block at a time. Then press. Seam allowances may be pressed to one side or open. If the quilted object is to receive much wear or if some fabric in the block is dark and some light, don't open the seam, but press it toward the darker of the two colors. That way the seam won't show through the light colored fabric and it will be stronger. If quilting close to the seam line through three layers of fabric is going to be too difficult, as it occasionally is with hand quilting, then press seams open.

After you've sewn and pressed all the blocks, compare them to make sure they're all the same size. If block sizes vary, adjust the seams wherever necessary to make them uniform.

Joining Blocks

"Setting together" means sewing the blocks together to form the quilt top or necessary yardage for the patchwork project you're working on. In patchwork, there's always a logical way to set the blocks together. If, for instance, your quilt top is made up of squares, the easiest way to assemble the top is to sew several blocks together to form a row, then sew the rows together to make up the completed top. If all blocks are uniform in size, this method should be no problem. But care must be taken in sewing the rows of blocks together so each block lines up precisely with the one next to it.

Arrange pieces for a project made up of squares or random colors and prints by laying all of them out on the floor and placing them in a pleasing relationship to each other. At this time, add alternate solid color blocks or stripes if you're using them. Borders should be added after all the blocks are joined together.

Making Borders

Borders are sewn to the completed quilt top in one of two ways, depending on how you want to finish the corners. If you're going to overlap the edges, pin the lengthwise strips to the quilt, right sides together, and machine-sew ¼ inch from the cut edges. Then do the same with the widthwise strips.

Mitering the corners is a bit trickier, but the professional-looking result is often worth the extra work. First pin the lengthwise border strips to the quilt, right sides together. Let the ends of the border extend beyond the quilt top a little more than the width of the strip. Machine-sew a ¼-inch seam. Next, pin the crosswise strips to the quilt top, but not to the lengthwise border strips. These strips should be longer than the quilt top is wide. Sew these border strips only to the quilt. Fold the crosswise border strip up so its right side faces the right side of the quilt. Fold the extension of the strip up at a 45-degree angle, then turn the folded crosswise border back down into normal position. Hand stitch the diagonal fold in place joining adjacent border strips.

Another way to form a quilt border is to turn the backing fabric to the front and then stitch it in place. Since this is done after the quilting has been completed, instructions for this method of making a border are given in the quilting basics section, starting on page 46.

Mile-a-Minute Machine Patchwork

This is the quickest and easiest way to make a checkerboard pattern. Here's how to do it:

1. Select two fabrics that are compatible in color or design, washability, and weight. Prewash the fabric and press it flat.

2. Lay out each piece of fabric on a smooth, flat surface. Using a yardstick and tailor's chalk, mark strips 3½ inches wide. Cut on the marked lines. Strips may be cut either with the grain of the fabric or across it.

3. With right sides together, join the strips lengthwise with ¼-inch seams. Alternate the prints or colors so that when all strips are sewn together, you have a "striped" piece of fabric. See top photo (A). Press seams open.

4. Lay the pieced fabric out so strips run crosswise in front of you. Using a yardstick and chalk, mark the fabric in strips 3½ inches wide. Cut on the lines. Handle the strips carefully to keep stitches from raveling. See middle photo.

5. Pin the strips together again, right sides facing. Reverse every other strip so that alternating blocks of fabric meet to form a checkerboard pattern. Pin the strips together carefully to be sure the seams between the patches meet.
meet.

6. Restitch the strips together, using a ¼-inch seam allowance. See bottom photo at right. To keep puckering at a minimum, stitch at a steady, even speed. Press all seams open.

7. For other less-symmetrical patchwork patterns, experiment with placement of strips for different effects.

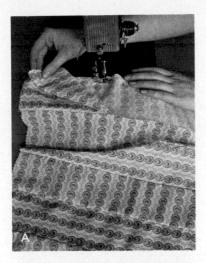

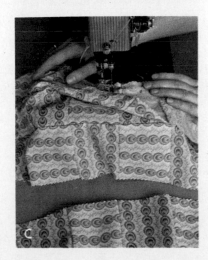

Quick and Easy Patchwork Place Mats

Patchwork place mats are a great way to use up odd scraps of fabrics left over from sewing. Since mats usually measure 12x18 or 20 inches, each piece can be quite small, giving you the chance to make use of even the tiniest bits of fabric. Combine a variety of prints and the mats will fit nicely into any table decorating scheme.

Materials
Pattern paper
Fabric for patches
1 yard 45-inch-wide cotton
   (lining for four mats)
1 yard polyester fleece
   (optional padding)

Directions
Cut a piece of paper 12x18 inches and mark it into six or eight large rectangles. Use a heavy wax pencil or a felt marker so the lines are bold. Then, within each rectangle, break the space up into smaller rectangles of different sizes. Number each small shape. On a second piece of the same size paper, make a tracing of the pattern to use as a guide while you are assembling the mat.

Cut the original pattern apart and use each piece as a cutting guide. Remember to add ¼-inch seam allowances to all sides of the pieces as you cut them. When all the pieces from one of the larger areas have been cut out, sew them together into a block. Press the seams and set the block aside. Repeat the same procedure for each of the other large blocks, referring to your pattern tracing whenever necessary. Then join the blocks together to form the finished top.

Cut a piece of lining fabric the same size as the pieced top. Stitch the lining to the top, right sides together, in a ¼-inch seam. Leave six inches open along one side for turning. For a padded mat, add a layer of fleece on top of the lining before sewing lining and top together. Then stitch as for an unpadded mat. Clip the corners of the mat, turn it right side out, and press. Slip-stitch the opening closed.

If you've padded the mat, you might want to machine stitch along the seams between the blocks to quilt it. This takes a little extra effort, but the result is a firmer place mat.

Quick and Easy Patchwork Tablecloth

If you can sew a straight seam, you can create this charming patchwork tablecloth. Four-inch squares come together in a hodgepodge of patterns in this practical and pretty bit of patchwork for your table. Add a demi-ruffle of eyelet for a touch of country elegance, then just see how well this table cover fits into any easygoing eating area.

Materials
Lightweight cardboard
Fabric for patches
Ruffled eyelet trim
Lining fabric

Directions
Make this patchwork tablecloth any desired size. First, decide on the finished size, then divide the width by four to determine how many squares wide your patchwork will be. Likewise, divide the length by four to find how many rows of squares you'll need. If necessary, add or subtract a few inches on length and width to make even multiples of four. Then make a cardboard template for cutting the squares.

Since the finished squares are 4x4 inches and you'll have to allow a ¼-inch seam allowance, cut a piece of cardboard 4½x4½ inches. If your cloth is large and requires a great number of squares, cut several templates. Then you can replace worn templates and avoid cutting blocks that aren't perfectly square. Place your fabric wrong side up, then lay on the template and trace around it. Cut along the penciled lines. If you're cutting squares from large lengths of fabric, you can avoid drawing every square by cutting a long 4½-inch-wide strip, then dividing the strip into 4½-inch squares.

Sew squares together to form rows, then sew the rows together to create the completed table cover. Pin ruffled eyelet to the edges, right sides together, and machine stitch ⅛ inch in from edge. Cut lining fabric to the finished size of the tablecloth. Place the lining and patchwork together, right sides facing and with the ruffle inside. Sew ¼ inch in all around the edges, leaving an opening on one side. Turn, press, and slip-stitch the opening closed.

Quick and Easy Patchwork Lounging Mat

A soft and sittable lounge mat like this one is as much at home indoors as it is out on the sun deck or patio. And it's a natural for children's summertime slumber parties too – comfortable, but lightweight and easy to tote almost anywhere.

Materials
1½ yards each of two solid colors and two complementary print fabrics
2 twin-size polyester quilt batts

Directions
Cut the fabric into thirty-four 6x36-inch strips. Sew pairs of strips together to form open-ended tubes. To do this, place two strips of fabric right sides together and pin securely. Sew up the long sides in ½-inch seams, but leave the short ends open. When you have completed 17 tubes, turn and press them and arrange them in an appealing sequence. Then overlap the adjoining long edges about ½ inch and topstitch them together. For a strong mat, sew two rows of stitches, each close to the folded edge, so the tubes are joined in what looks like a flat-fell seam.

Cut pieces of polyester batting 15x36 inches, and fold each one in thirds lengthwise. Pull a roll of batting through each tube to stuff the mat. Then machine baste across the ends of the tubes, being sure to catch the batting in the stitching. Trim the fabric and the batting close to the basting stitches.

Make long ties to hold the mat when it's rolled up. First, cut four strips of fabric approximately 6x50 inches. Then sew pairs of strips together, right sides facing, and make a diagonal seam across one end. Leave the other end open. Turn and press.

Open the long seam five inches in the center of one of the end tubes of the mat. Insert the raw edges of the ties and topstitch the seam closed. Bind the edges of the mat with 2½-inch-wide strips of one of the fabrics used for the tubes.

Quick and Easy Patchwork Chair Pad

For a room with several pretty prints, why not create a patchwork chair pad to bring them all together in a delightful medley of patterns? For the contemporary rocker featured at left, blue and white print fabrics combine nicely to provide the chair with a custom cover that's easy to stitch—and economical, too. This same style patching can work wonders in rejuvenating a favorite antique chair as well.

Materials
Assorted prints for patchwork
Solid color fabric for backing
Heavy canvas
Polyester quilt batting
  or fleece

Directions
To start your chair pad, determine the size of the sling. Then cut a piece of heavy canvas to this size, adding five extra inches on each end for fitting over the frame and tacking down.

Plan your patchwork top so it will be the same length but one inch wider than the canvas. Decide on the size of your squares and make a template for them, adding ¼-inch seam allowance if you wish. Cut squares of print fabrics and sew them together into rows. Then stitch the rows together to form the cover.

Cut a piece of backing fabric the same size as the finished patchwork. Cut a layer of polyester fleece or quilt batting the same size as the canvas. For more padding, cut several layers.

Place the backing fabric on the floor, wrong side up. Lay the canvas on top of it, and the padding over the canvas. Then add the top, right side up. Baste all layers together. Quilt or tie the layers together. For quilting, machine stitch along the seams between the squares. Use a heavy needle and stitch slowly so as not to break or bend the needle. For tying, use pearl cotton threaded into a needle. Take a small stitch through all layers in the corners of the squares. Knot the threads and cut off the excess.

To finish the edges, fold the top over the canvas, then fold under the edge of the backing. Slip-stitch the side edges closed. Machine stitch along the edges, and attach cover to the frame.

Quick and Easy Patchwork Quilt and Shams

There's nothing more traditional-looking than a patchwork quilt made of squares and triangles. And the very nicest part of the quilt shown here is that it's not nearly as difficult as it may seem. The secret is to sew four triangles to each square, forming a large block. Once the blocks are sewn, the quilt top is pieced exactly as if you were working with single squares. It's the arrangement of colors and prints that makes a quilt like this so spectacular.

Materials
3 yards 45-inch-wide
  black print fabric
3½ yards 45-inch-wide
  green fabric
4¼ yards 45-inch-wide
  white fabric
7 yards backing fabric
Yellow knitting worsted
Polyester batting

Directions
To create the quilt you see here, cut 29 10-inch squares of black print fabric. Cut six 10-inch squares of green fabric. From white fabric, cut 72 triangles measuring 7x7x10 inches. Cut 68 triangles of the same size from green fabric. The measurements given above do not include seam allowances, so cut ¼ inch extra on all edges.

Sew triangles on each side of a square to form blocks. You'll need 17 blocks with black print squares and green triangles; 12 blocks with black print squares and white triangles; and six blocks with green squares and white triangles.

Sew four separate rows of five blocks alternating black and white blocks with black and green blocks. Start and end with black and white blocks. Sew three rows of five blocks alternating black and green blocks with green and white blocks. Start and end these rows with black and green blocks.

Sew rows in alternate color schemes together to form the completed quilt top. Piece backing fabric to the right size and assemble the top, batting, and backing according to the instructions on page 47. With yellow washable knitting worsted, tie the layers together where the green and white triangles meet.

To make pillow shams or covers, decrease the size of the squares and triangles. For a snug-fitting cover, cut squares 4¼x4¼ inches (add seam allowances) and triangles 3x3x4¼ inches. For a loose-fitting cover, cut squares 5x5 inches, and triangles 3½x3½x5 inches.

Cut 12 squares and 48 triangles. Make each cover with three rows of four blocks each. Assemble the covers in the same way as the quilt. Use backing fabric for backs of covers.

Quick and Easy Checkerboard Quilt

There are few things faster to make than a checkerboard quilt. Simply follow instructions on page 9 for our mile-a-minute machine patchwork and you can whip up this red and white beauty in no time. Even if you've never pieced before, try this quilt.

Materials
2½ yards 45-inch-wide red fabric
2½ yards 45-inch-wide white fabric
One sheet or six yards backing fabric
Polyester quilt batting

Directions
Start by preshrinking and pressing all the fabric. Be sure the lengthwise and crosswise grains are straight and at right angles to each other. Next, cut the fabric into strips 4½ inches wide and sew the strips together, alternating colors. The seam allowance is ¼ inch. Press the seams open.

Cut the "striped" fabric into strips 4½ inches wide across the existing seams. Reverse the strips and sew them back together to form the checkerboard pattern. Assemble the quilt according to the instructions beginning on page 46.

Quick and Easy Patchwork Curtain

Here's a free-style patchwork curtain–ideal as a laundry cover-up, pictured at left, and as a cheerful shower curtain, too. If you're after a quick and easy project with big impact and little effort–this curtain is a natural. Fabrics are arranged in a pleasing random style, such as that used in old-fashioned crazy quilting. For beginning patchers, here's a project to test your skills–with a hint of appliqué added just for the fun of it.

Materials
Assorted print fabrics
One sheet or fabric for backing
Metal grommets (optional)

Directions
Measure the size of your doorway or shower, and draw a diagram to scale on which to work out your pattern. Plan the design in vertical strips of varying widths. Next, divide the strips into uneven rectangles. Cut the fabric and piece the strips; then add an appliqué heart or two, and sew the strips together into a curtain. Cut and piece fabric for a backing the same size as the curtain. Place the two right sides together and sew, leaving an opening for turning. Turn and stitch the opening closed. Add fabric loops at the top for hanging or metal grommets for hooks.

Quick and Easy Patchwork Coverlets

A bedspread or coverlet can be as easy as sewing big squares of fabric together. And in the case of the patchwork on the opposite page, the squares don't even have to be cut. They're big bandannas sewn together —blue on one side, red on the other, to make the coverlet reversible.

Materials
Fabric patches for coverlet top, this page
Sheet or backing fabric for coverlet, this page
Red and blue bandannas for coverlet top and back, opposite
Quilt batting
Yarn for tying (optional)

Directions
Blocks for the quilt above will be 10 inches square when finished, so determine the number you need for the finished quilt size you want. First, cut fabric squares 10½x10½ inches. Arrange the blocks in a pleasing pattern, and then sew them together in rows, using ¼-inch seam allowances. Sew rows together to form the completed top. For the backing, use a sheet in a complementary color, or piece lengths of fabric to the size of the top. Assemble backing, batting, and top according to quilting directions beginning on page 46. Either tie the coverlet in the corners of the blocks or quilt around them to hold the batting in place.

The bandanna quilt, pictured opposite, requires 18 large squares of each color placed three across and six down for a twin bed. To make a double-bed quilt, use 24 bandannas placed four across and six down. If you use bandannas smaller than 18x18 inches, adjust the number needed to achieve the desired coverlet size.

Using ¼-inch seam allowances, stitch all the blue bandannas together, then all the red ones. As in all patchwork, stitch blocks into rows, and then stitch the rows together to form the completed coverlet top or backing.

For an especially puffy quilt, cut four layers of quilt batting the same size as the seamed bandannas. Lay one cover on the floor, wrong side up. Top with the layers of batting and the other cover, right side up. Pin or baste the batting and fabrics together to keep them from slipping. Fold under the outer blue and red edges ¼ inch and pin. Using large stitches and two colors of thread, stitch close to the edge. Tie the comforter at intervals with red, white, or blue yarn, or machine quilt with two colors of thread.

Quick and Easy Patchwork Comforter

One of the easiest ways to create the soft, inviting look of a puffy comforter is to make the quilt of separate little pillows, each stuffed to give you the degree of "puff" you're after. The quilt on this page shows you one method of making a pre-stuffed cover. On the next page is still another way to achieve the same charming effect.

Materials

Fabric patches in sufficient
   quantity for desired
   size quilt
Pillow stuffing or batting

Directions

When determining quilt size, be sure the dimensions are divisible by a number that gives you a comfortable size pillow to work with. For example, the length and width of your quilt should be divisible by four if you want a quilt made of four-inch pillows.

To make each pillow, cut fabric the same width and twice the length of the planned pillow, plus the ¼-inch seam allowances. So, for a 4-inch pillow, cut fabric 4½x8½ inches. Fold the fabric in half, right sides together. Sew two sides and part of the third. Clip the corners and turn. Make sure corners are fully pushed out and square.

Stuff pillows with pillow stuffing or one or more layers of quilt batting cut to size. Then turn under the raw edges and slip-stitch the opening closed. Make as many pillows as you need for your quilt.

Assemble the quilt first by laying the pillows on the floor in an attractive arrangement. Then make a squared diagram on paper, assigning numbers to each square to represent a pillow. Pin numbered pieces of paper to the pillows and store them in a convenient place as you work. When you're ready for a pillow, find the one with the right number and sew it in its assigned place.

Join pillows by slip-stitching. Overlap the edges of two pillows ³/₈-inch and stitch across the top surface, then turn the pillows over and sew across the back. Two rows of stitching are needed to make the quilt strong and durable.

Once the quilt begins to take shape, decide which surface will be the top so the stitching is consistent—first across the top, then the back. When all the pillows are sewn together, the quilt is finished.

Quick and Easy Patchwork Pillow Quilt

Make this pillow quilt with pillow tops and backs of different sizes. This accounts for the fullness of the loose-puff look you see here.

Materials

Assorted print fabric for 12-inch squares
Muslin for 11-inch squares
Fabric for quilt backing
Pillow stuffing or quilt batting

Below left: Pinning corners and tucks
Below right: Catching tucks in stitching

Directions

To make this quilt, begin by cutting muslin or background squares 11½x11½ inches. Cut assorted print fabrics into 12½-inch squares. For a king-size bed such as the one pictured at right, you'll need 132 finished pillows sewn into 12 rows of 11 pillows each. For a double bed, you need to make 90 pillows, arranged nine across and 10 long. Measurements of the squares include ¼-inch seam allowances.

Start construction of your pillow bedspread by pinning the top print fabric square to the smaller muslin square as shown in the left drawing below. Place pins in all four corners, then make tucks to take up the excess fabric along each edge. Sew around three sides of the pillow, leaving the fourth side open for stuffing. Trim corners and turn pillows right side out.

Use either polyester fiberfill or quilt batting to add the desired fullness to the pillows. If using quilt batting, cut as many layers as needed to get the amount of puff you want in each pillow. Cut batting slightly larger than the size of the square so it will fluff up inside pillows. When the stuffing has been added, turn under the raw edges ¼ inch along the opening, and finish sewing up the fourth side. Complete all pillows before sewing the bedspread.

Assemble the spread by first laying out the pillows on the floor in a pleasing arrangement of colors and patterns. Make a squared, numbered diagram on paper as a sewing guide, and pin slips of paper with the appropriate numbers to the pillows. Then sew pillows together in rows. Place two pillows together, right sides facing, and machine stitch with a ¼-inch seam allowance. Make sure the stitching line is inside the stitches used to construct the pillow.

When rows of pillows are completed, join the rows to form the completed top. Cut backing fabric to the right size and sew to the edges of the bedspread. Finish the edges with bias tape. Tie the pillows to keep the stuffing from shifting, or leave them loose for the draped-pillow look shown.

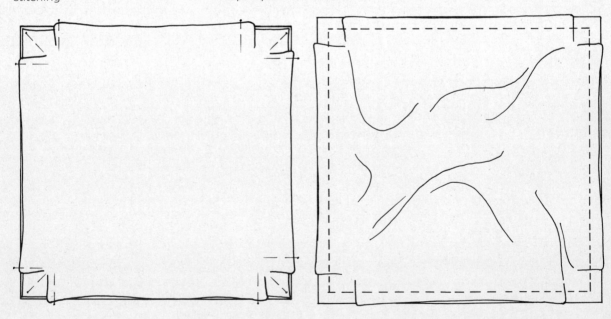

Quick and Easy Patchwork for Beginners

(shown on pages 4 and 5)

Everything shown on pages 4 and 5 is easily within your creative reach, even if you've never done patchwork before. The secret is to start with a simple project and gradually work up to more complex designs. But here are instructions for projects you can accomplish with ease.

Patchwork Quilt

This colorful quilt is a snap. First, decide on the size of the finished quilt, then determine how many squares to cut by dividing that measurement by three or four—the size of your squares. When cutting any kind of patchwork, be sure to add ¼-inch seam allowances to all measurements.

Lay out your patchwork squares on the floor and arrange them in a color and pattern placement that appeals to you. Then sew squares together to form rows. When all the rows are finished, sew them together for the completed quilt top. Use a sheet for backing fabric, or cut and piece yard goods to the proper size. When the backing is ready and pressed, lay it on the floor, wrong side up. Cover it first with quilt batting and put your completed quilt top on it, right side up. Pin and baste according to the instructions on page 47.

The quilt we show on pages 4 and 5 has been machine quilted. Instructions for this method of quilting appear on page 48. Follow them and quilt your project with diagonal lines through each square from corner to corner. When the quilting is done, the edges of the quilt may be finished in whatever method you

choose. One of the simplest ways for beginners to finish quilt edges is to sew wide bias tape to the quilt top, right sides together. Trim excess batting and backing, and turn the tape to the back side. Slip-stitch down.

Hearts and Flowers Pillow

What a fitting name for the 16-inch pillow diagrammed below. It's created from small-print floral fabric with a heart appliqué added to the center block.

To make this pillow, enlarge the pattern below. Then gather your materials, being sure all fabrics you select are preshrunk and pressed wrinkle-free.

When cutting fabrics, remember the ¼-inch seam allowance on all edges.

Cut each piece of the patch-

work according to the drawing below, then assemble. First, machine appliqué the heart to the large light colored square in the center of the pillow.

Then add the two print pieces to the sides of the center square, and sew on the top and bottom pieces. For the next fabric border, sew the top and bottom strips to the pillow, then add the two side pieces.

For the outside border, sew the small squares to each end of two of the strips and set aside. Sew the remaining outer strips to the sides of the pillow top. Then add the strips and squares to the top and bottom of the pillow. Make sure the squares line up with the strips at the sides. Press all seams open.

Cut backing fabric the size of the pillow cover. Place the two

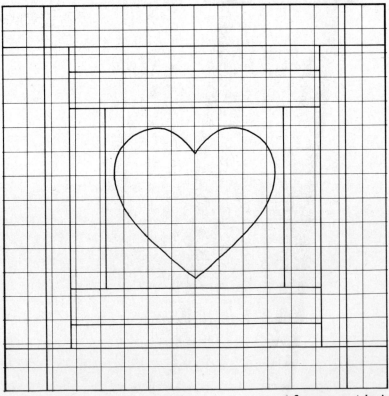

1 Square = 1 Inch

together, right sides facing, and sew on three sides. Clip the corners and turn the pillow cover right side out. Press lightly.

Insert a foam pillow form through the opening in the cover. Fold under the raw edges of the opening, pin closed, and sew edges together with neat slip-stitches.

School House Pillow

To create a project that has great effect for a minimum of effort, make this attractive design. This famous patchwork-appliqué pattern is twice as easy if you machine appliqué the design to the pillow top.

Start by enlarging the pattern below. Cut out a paper pattern and lay it on the appliqué fabric. Then trace around the pattern on the right side of the fabric. When cutting appliqué, be sure to include a ¼-inch turn-under allowance on all edges.

Cut the background fabric to the desired size and center the appliqué design on the pillow top. Pin and baste securely. Complete instructions for machine appliqué are given on page 65. Follow them to complete the appliqué of the schoolhouse.

To make the ruffle, cut a strip of fabric twice the width of the finished ruffle and add ½ inch for seams. The fabric strip should be twice as long as the total of the four sides of the pillow.

Fold the strip in half lengthwise, wrong sides together. Then, follow the instructions given on page 53; gather and join the strip. Pin the ruffle to the pillow top so the raw edges of the ruffle line up with the raw edges of the pillow top. Sew in place.

Cut the pillow back the same size as the top. Lay on top of the pillow cover and the ruffle, right sides together, and sew on three sides only. Make sure the ruffle is inside and doesn't get caught in the seam. Clip the corners and turn the cover right side out. Insert a foam pillow form and stitch opening closed.

Patchwork Place Mats

Place mats can be as simple or as complex as you want to make them. For openers, keep the patchwork easy. One of the mats shown on pages 4 and 5 is nothing more than two rectangular strips of print fabric sewn together in an L-shape and appliquéd to a floral print place mat.

The second of the place mats features several more rectangular strips joined in "log cabin" fashion. Though it looks complicated, it doesn't have to be.

Start with a center square or rectangle. Add pieces to the sides, top and bottom. Continue this procedure until your patchwork has reached the size you desire.

If you find your patchwork is square and you want to create a rectangular place mat, simply add vertical strips to either side to change the shape from square to rectangular.

When sewing place mats, remember they should be lined. Any patchwork project that will be washed repeatedly should have a backing fabric to keep the raw edges from raveling. You might also want to pad your place mats with a layer of batting or fleece.

Napkins can add still more color to your patchwork place mats. If you piece them, be sure to line them, too. Or, you may simply hem squares of print fabric coordinated with the place mats.

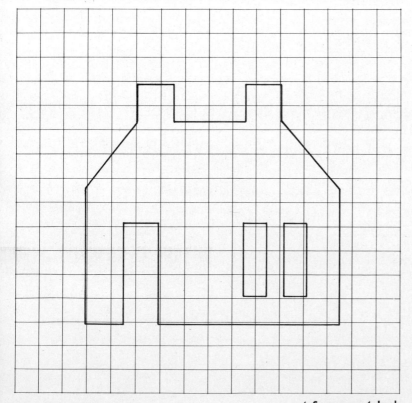

1 Square=1 Inch

Pieced Patchwork—

A Kaleidoscope of Patterns

For several hundred years now, quilters have been putting together bits of fabric to come up with new and different patterns each time they "pieced." One small change in the arrangement of the pieces—or in the color relationship of the pieces—and a brand-new design emerged. And it's this chameleon-like quality about patchwork that has kept it from becoming static. Today, it's still exciting, still challenging—and one of the most satisfying forms of fabric art you'll ever attempt. Here you see pieced patchwork featuring many of the famous patterns, plus some new variations of old designs. Small blocks of patchwork are used for pot holders, larger pieces for place mats and pillow covers—and some designs are executed as wall hangings. Just as there's no end to patchwork patterns, there's no end to what you can do with the pieced patchwork you make. Complete instructions for all projects shown on these two pages begin on page 28.

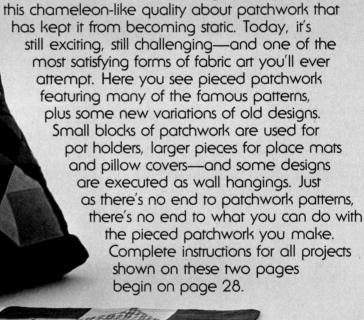

A Kaleidoscope of Patterns—Attic Windows

Attic Windows is a versatile and easy-to-piece pattern that adapts beautifully to a variety of projects. The scale and repeat of the pattern are suitable for small projects like pillows and place mats, but are equally effective on larger projects such as curtains and quilts. The handsome framed wall hanging shown on page 27 and detailed in the diagram at right is composed of 20 four-inch-square Attic Window blocks arranged in five rows of four blocks each.

Materials
¼ yard 45-inch-wide fabric in
   colors A, B, and C
16x20-inch double-weight
   poster board
Fabric glue
16x20-inch picture frame

Attic Windows

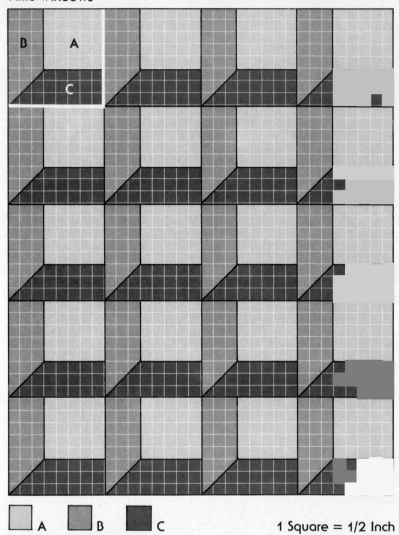

A B C

1 Square = 1/2 Inch

Directions
Enlarge the above pattern to size, and cut 20 squares from fabric A. Cut 20 pieces each of fabrics B and C. Be sure to add a ¼-inch seam allowance around all pattern pieces.

Construct 20 blocks by sewing color B along one side of the square of fabric A. Then add the C piece to form a four-inch square. Press seams open. Join four squares together in a row. Make five rows and join them together to form the completed hanging. Apply fabric glue to the outer ¼-inch edges of the poster board and to the seam allowances where the blocks are joined. With the patchwork face down on a hard, clean, smooth surface, center the glued side of the board and press it in place. Insert the patchwork-covered board in the 16x20-inch frame and hang.

Joseph's Coat

Joseph's Coat

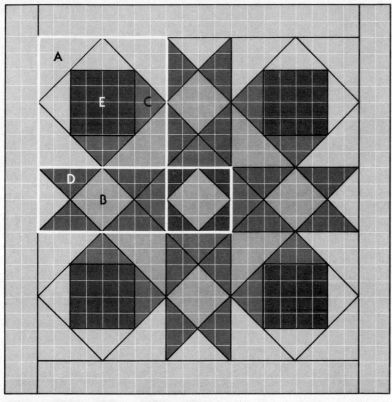

☐ A ▨ B ▩ C ▦ D ■ E   1 Square=1 Inch

Joseph's Coat is a striking pattern composed entirely of triangles and squares. The piecing of one 20-inch-square block of this pattern is intricate and requires precision stitching, but even a single completed block has great impact when mounted on the front of a 24-inch square pillow. (Shown at far left on page 26.)

Materials

1½ yards 45-inch fabric in
  color A
Scraps of fabrics B, C, D, E
24-inch pillow form
Quilt batting

Directions

Enlarge and follow the above diagram for pattern pieces and color placement. Cut all pieces with ¼-inch seam allowances. Start assembling pillow top by sewing two small A triangles and two C triangles to each of the four E squares, making larger squares. To each of these, sew three large A triangles and one B triangle. (Check diagram for placement.) To one B square, add the four E triangles and set aside. Next, piece four rectangular blocks consisting of six triangles and one B square. Join all the assembled blocks to form the "Joseph's coat" pattern shown here. To opposite sides of the finished square, add the shorter border strips, then add the longer ones.

Pin the completed top to a 21x21-inch piece of batting and quilt according to instructions beginning on page 46. Padding is smaller than the pillow top, so center it carefully. Outline quilt on all of the color B pieces and the color E squares. Cut a piece of backing 25x25 inches from fabric A. Attach the backing to the pillow top, right sides together. Leave an 18-inch opening on one side for turning. Do not clip corners. Instead, make a box seam two inches deep at each corner. Turn the pillow right side out and insert a 24-inch pillow form. Blindstitch the opening closed.

A Kaleidoscope of Patterns—Lisa's Choice
(continued)

Lisa's Choice is the traditional pattern used in the 16-inch-square wall hanging shown in the upper left-hand corner of page 27. Worked predominantly in two shades of one color (greens, in our sample), the star portion of the pattern takes on a strong dimensional effect. The basic pieced unit may be repeated any number of times to make a pillow, a tablecloth, or a quilt. For example, 20 of these 16-inch square blocks will yield a quilt approximately 64x80 inches (four units wide by five units long).

Materials
Scraps of fabric in five colors
½ yard fabric for backing and
   hanging loops
Quilt Batting

Lisa's Choice

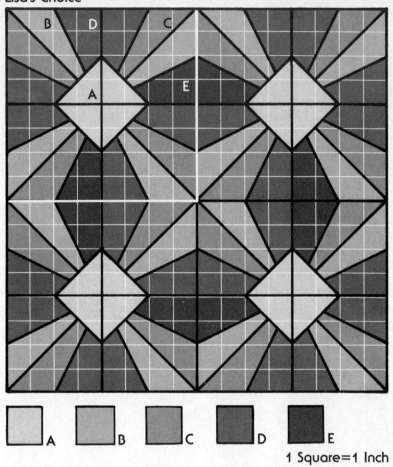

1 Square=1 Inch

Directions
Enlarge the drawing to size and make a template for each shape. Add seam allowances. Cut 16 triangles in color A and 16 pieces each in B and C. Cut 24 D pieces. Cut four E pieces, then reverse the pattern and cut four more E pieces so you have four right-side and four left-side shapes. To piece Lisa's Choice, join B and C pieces along the long side. To eight of these pairs, add D to both the B and C sides. To four, add a D piece to the C side and an E to the B side. To four, add a D to the B side and an E to the C side. Now add an A triangle to each group to form four-inch squares. Arrange the blocks according to the diagram and piece four squares together into a row. Make four rows, then join the four rows to complete the basic block.

To make the block into a wall hanging, cut a piece of batting 17x17 inches and a piece of backing fabric the same size. Cut three hanging loops twice the desired width and length of the finished folded loop, plus seam allowances. Fold in half lengthwise. Stitch and turn. Press and position loops on patchwork face. Join pieced top, batting, and backing according to instructions beginning on page 46.

Galaxy

Galaxy

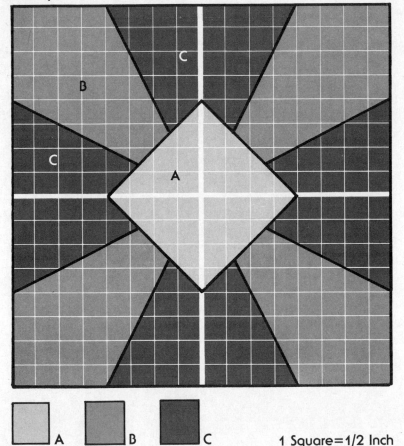

A B C   1 Square=1/2 Inch

The Galaxy pattern shown at left is another traditional quilt pattern that is equally handsome when used as a single block, or repeated across the length and breadth of a whole quilt. The pattern may be executed in solids (as illustrated in the rust, brown and green pot holder shown in the lower left-hand corner on page 26), but would look particularly striking pieced in a combination of prints and solids.

Materials
Scraps of fabric in three colors
of your choice
¼ yard fabric for backing and
loop
Quilt batting or polyester fleece

Directions
Enlarge the diagram to size and transfer the pattern pieces to paper or lightweight cardboard. Cut four triangles of color A and four pattern pieces of B. Cut eight pieces of C, four on the right side of the fabric, then reverse the pattern and cut four more so you have right-side and left-side pieces. Cut all pieces with a ¼-inch seam allowance.

Join the pieces by sewing a left- and a right-hand piece in color C to each side of the four pieces of color B. To these add a triangle, A, forming a four-inch square. Join the four squares according to the above diagram to form one block of the Galaxy pattern.

To make the block into a pot holder, cut 9x9-inch squares of fleece or quilt batting and of backing fabric. Baste patchwork to batting or fleece. Cut a 1x4-inch fabric strip for a loop. Fold it lengthwise, right sides together, and stitch. Turn the loop and pin it to a corner on the right side of the top. Stitch top to backing fabric, right sides together. Leave an opening for turning. Trim padding close to the seam line. Turn the pot holder and slip-stitch the opening closed. Quilt the pot holder following the instructions beginning on page 46.

A Kaleidoscope of Patterns—Seven Old Favorites
(continued)

Magic Cubes 1 Square = 1 Inch

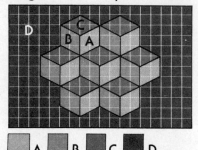

☐ A ■ B ■ C ■ D

King's Cross 1 Square = 3/4 Inch

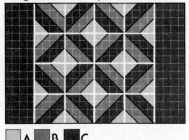

☐ A ■ B ■ C

Sister's Choice 1 Square = 1 Inch

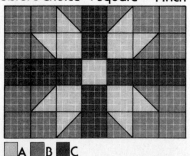

☐ A ■ B ■ C

Rivoli Cross 1 Square = 3/4 Inch

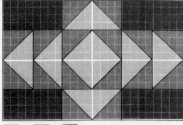

☐ A ■ B ■ C

Here's an assortment of popular pieced patterns to add to your patchwork repertoire.

Magic Cubes

This pattern is a natural as an appliqué for a place mat (as shown on page 26) or for many other interesting projects. Enlarge the diagram and cut the pieces from colors of your choice. Be sure to add ¼-inch seam allowances.

Start by sewing the color A diamonds to the color B diamonds. Add the C diamonds to form seven hexagons. Then join the hexagons to form one large "magic cube" patch: Starting with a center hexagon, add the others clockwise.

Cut two pieces of D background fabric 14x20 inches. Cut batting to match. Center the patchwork on one piece of background fabric and machine-appliqué according to instructions on page 65. Baste the appliquéd top and batting together. Then sew backing to top, right sides together, leaving an opening for turning. Trim batting, turn, and press. Slip-stitch the opening closed. Outline quilt following the instructions on page 50.

King's Cross

For a striking place mat (shown on page 26), enlarge the diagram at left and cut 32 triangles of color A and 16 trapezoids each of B and C. Cut two 3¾x12¾-inch pieces of fabric C. Cut backing and batting 13x19 inches.

First join the B and C trapezoids along their long bases. Add an A triangle to the top of each trapezoid, forming a three-inch square. Arrange the squares in rows of four, so B and C trapezoids touch, then piece rows to form a 12-inch square. Add C strips to two sides, completing the top. Baste top and batting, and then stitch top to back, right sides together, leaving an opening for turning. Trim batting, turn, and slip-stitch closed. Machine-quilt according to instructions on page 50.

Sister's Choice

To make the patchwork bath mat shown on page 27, first enlarge the pattern at left. Then cut eight triangles each of colors A and B, five squares of A, 12 of B, and 10 of C. Cut batting and backing 21x29 inches.

Join pieces by sewing A triangles to B triangles to form squares. Follow the diagram and piece seven rows of five squares each. Join rows to complete the bath mat top. Press seams open.

Baste the completed top to the batting. Place the backing fabric on the bath mat top, right sides together, and stitch around the edges, leaving an opening. Trim batting close to stitching. Turn and slip-stitch opening closed.

Following instructions on page 50, outline-quilt the five areas of color A and the four rectangles of color C.

Rivoli Cross

A single unit of this pattern also makes a lovely place mat (see page 26). Enlarge the diagram at lower left and cut pattern pieces, adding seam allowances. Cut backing and batting to 13x19 inches.

Join the long side of each B triangle to the short sides of each A triangle to form rectangles, then sew two pairs of these into 6-inch squares. To each square, attach the C rectangles to make the ends of the mat. Then sew two rectangles along the long sides of the A triangles to form the center of the mat. Add remaining rectangles to each side of the center. Join side sections to center. Attach backing as for other place mats.

Hexagon Flower

While this pattern makes an interesting quilt, a single hexagon flower is charming as a pot holder. To make one, enlarge the diagram at upper right and make patterns for the pieces, adding ¼-inch seam allowances.

Cut six hexagons in color A and one in color B. Cut six diamonds in color C. Use one of the three colors for backing and cut this piece and batting approximately 9x10 inches.

Piece the six color A hexagons to the B hexagon, one at a time, working in a clockwise direction. Add the six C diamonds to complete the top. Make a hanging loop of the fabric you've chosen for the backing.

Pin and baste together the pieced top and the batting. Place the loop on the right side of the pot holder with the raw edges of the loop lined up with the raw edges of the top. Then place the backing fabric on the patchwork, right sides together. Sew around the edges, leaving an opening for turning. Trim batting close to seam line, turn, and slip-stitch the opening.

Machine-quilt along the outlines of the pieces, following the instructions on page 50.

Hexagon Star

To make the pillow shown on page 27, enlarge the drawing at center right and make patterns for the pieces. Cut six triangles of color A, six of B, and 12 of C. Cut 12 trapezoids of color A, six of B, and six of C. Cut with ¼-inch seam allowances. Cut batting and backing fabric to 20x 21 inches.

Piece the triangles to the shorter base of the trapezoids as follows: B triangles to C trapezoids; C triangles to A trapezoids; A triangles to B trapezoids. Join the resulting triangles in rows following the diagram,

then join the rows together to complete the top.

Baste the completed top to a piece of batting and quilt the two layers. Follow the quilting instructions beginning on page 46. The pillow shown has concentric rows of quilting ³/₈-inch apart to fill the two central hexagonal areas. After quilting, complete the pillow by joining the backing fabric to the front. Place the two, right sides together, and stitch around the edges, leaving an opening for turning; turn. Stuff with pillow stuffing. Stitch the opening closed.

Rolling Star

To make a pillow top of this popular pattern (like the one shown on page 27), enlarge the diagram at lower right. Make templates for the pattern pieces using ¼ inch seam allowances.

Cut eight diamonds from striped fabric and eight diamonds of color A. Cut eight squares and four triangles of color B. Cut two pieces of B 2¼x14 inches. Cut two pieces of A 2¼x14 inches, and two pieces 2¼x15½ inches. Cut pieces of muslin lining and backing fabric 16 inches square.

Piece the striped diamonds together to form an eight-pointed star. Add the color B squares as shown. Next, add color A diamonds, then add the triangles to form a large square. Sew the border pieces of color B to the outside edges. Repeat with color A border pieces to complete pillow top.

Pin the top right side up, to a piece of muslin, and round the corners. If desired, sew piping to the right side of the top. Place backing fabric on pillow top, right sides together. Sew around edges, leaving an opening for turning. Clip corners, turn, and press. Stuff with polyester fiberfill and stitch opening closed.

Flower **1 Square = 1 Inch**

![Flower diagram]

A   B   C

Hexagon Star 1 Square = 1 Inch

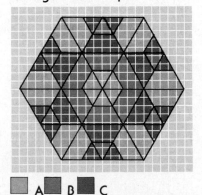

A   B   C

Rolling Star 1 Square = 1 Inch

A   B

Star Pattern Tablecloth or Quilt Top

Star patterns are probably the most popular of all patchwork designs. The one used on this table cover is the famous Ohio Star, made of nine-patch blocks separated by white strips. This design works well for many patchwork projects, including quilts.

Materials

2¾ yards 45-inch-wide white cotton

2¼ yards 45-inch-wide printed cotton

1³/₈ yards 45-inch-wide blue cotton

½ yard 45-inch-wide red cotton

1 full-size white sheet for backing

Quilt batting (optional)

Directions

For each nine-patch block of the Ohio Star tablecloth, cut four 3½-inch print squares and one 3½-inch blue square. Cut eight 4¼x3x3-inch triangles of blue and eight of print fabric.

To make each block, stitch four print triangles to the sides of a blue center square. Stitch two blue triangles to adjacent sides of each print square. Right sides together, pin blue triangles on each square to print triangles on each side of the center square. Stitch. Sew the four remaining print triangles to the blue triangles to complete the block. Press seams toward the blue fabric.

Cut 36 4x10-inch white strips. For each row, join seven blocks and six strips, starting and ending with blocks. Make six rows of blocks. Cut five 4x87-inch strips of white fabric. Sew together alternate rows of blocks and long strips. Use ¼-inch seam allowances on all seams.

To make border strips, cut two 2x72-inch and two 2x84½-inch blue strips. Cut two 2x75-inch and two 2x90½-inch print strips. Cut two 3½x78-inch and two 3½x93½-inch red strips. Pin and sew on blue, print, and red borders, forming butt corners. Padding and quilting are optional. To quilt, follow directions beginning on page 46. Otherwise, simply join to backing cut or pieced to size.

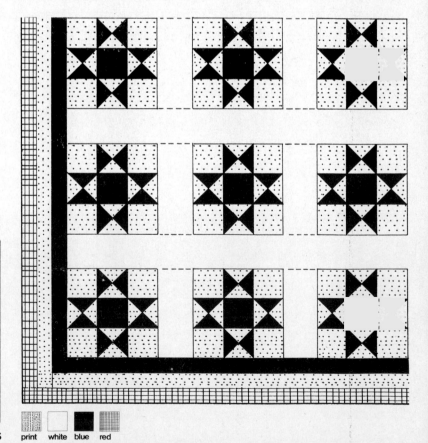

Below: Ohio Star pattern
Right: Tablecloth or quilt top

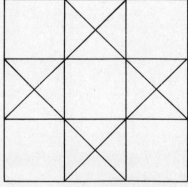

1 Square = 3 Inches

print white blue red

Star Pattern Curtains and Pillow

Want a big-impact project for your home? Then patch a star, like our saw-tooth pattern or classic eight-point design at right. Curtains give you plenty of patchwork charm, without being as time-consuming to make as a quilt or tablecloth. Better yet for a quickie project—try a dazzling star pillow like the one featured at right.

Materials

Cafe Curtains (See *Note.*)
3 yards orange border print
1 yard dark green print
1¾ yards yellow fabric
1 yard striped fabric
1 yard light green
3½ yards lightweight white
  cotton (lining)

Pillow
¼ yard striped fabric
¼ yard dark green print
¼ yard light green print
¾ yard orange print
¼ yard yellow fabric
1 14- or 16-inch pillow form

Directions

Saw-tooth Star Curtains

Note: Yardage given is for four 30x30-inch panels. To change measurements, adjust the width of the border strips, add blocks of patchwork, or reduce the size of the pieces within a block.

Enlarge the diagram below and cut square and triangular templates for fabric patches. Preshrink the fabric before cutting. Using the diagram as a cutting and placement guide, cut out fabric pieces. Be sure to add ¼-inch seam allowances to edges before cutting.

Sew triangles together to form squares, then stitch squares together into rows as in the diagram. Press. Stitch rows together into a block, matching crosswise seams. For each panel, join four blocks, using 2½-inch-wide strips of border fabric to separate them. Join the blocks two at a time with a 12½-inch-long strip, then join the two sets of blocks with a 26½-inch-long strip.

Cut a piece of lining fabric the same size as the four-block section and baste it to the blocks. Then, cut two strips of border fabric 4½x26½ inches and stitch them to two opposite sides of the panel. Then cut two 4½x30½-inch strips and sew them to the remaining sides. Fold the border over the raw edges of the panel, turn under ¼ inch, and slip-stitch to the back of the panel.

Eight-point Star Pillow

Enlarge the diagram below and cut square and triangular templates for fabric patches. Using the diagram as a cutting and placement guide, cut out fabric pieces. For the border of a 16-inch pillow, cut two pieces 2½x16½ inches and two pieces 2½x12½ inches. To make a 14-inch pillow, cut strips 1½ inches wide instead.

Sew triangles together into squares. Press. Then lay out all the squares in rows to form the design shown in the drawing. Stitch pieces together one row at a time and press. Then join rows together, matching crosswise seams. Press. Stitch border pieces to block as indicated in the diagram. Back completed pillow top with yellow fabric, insert the pillow, and slip-stitch the cover closed.

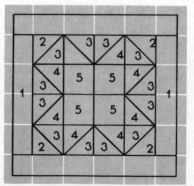

Saw-tooth Star

KEY   1 Square = 3 Inches
1 = Border Print   4 = Stripe
2 = Dk Green Print 5 = Lt Green Print
3 = Yellow

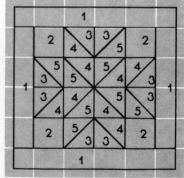

Eight-point Star

KEY   1 Square = 3 Inches
1 = Border Stripe   4 = Orange Print
2 = Dk Green Print 5 = Yellow
3 = Lt Green Print

Right: Saw-tooth Star pattern
Far Right: Eight-point Star pattern

Star Pattern Quilt and Pillow Sham

Parading the colors has never been done more effectively than in this red, white, and blue star pattern quilt with matching pillow shams. Its finished size is about 80x96 inches.

Materials

Quilt
3 yards 36-inch red fabric
4 yards 36-inch white fabric
1¼ yards 45-inch small red and white polka dot fabric
1¼ yards 45-inch small blue and white polka dot fabric
¾ yard 45-inch large blue and white polka dot fabric
6 yards 45-inch backing fabric
Full-size quilt batting
Red, white, or blue embroidery floss (optional)

Pillow Sham
(Directions are on page 43.)
12x15 inches red fabric
¾ yard white fabric
9x14 inches small red and white polka dot fabric
9x14 inches small blue and white polka dot fabric
13x22 inches large blue and white polka dot fabric
²/₃ yard red, white, or blue backing fabric

Directions

Star Pattern Quilt
Draw the patterns shown below on sandpaper or lightweight cardboard and cut out to use as templates for the quilt pattern pieces. The ¼-inch seam allowance is included in the dimensions given for the pieces.

Preshrink and press your fabric before you begin measuring and cutting. Straighten the grain of the fabric and be sure lengthwise and crosswise threads are at right angles to each other. When marking fabric for cutting, line up the sides of the squares and the right-angle sides of the triangles with the straight grain of the fabric. On the diamonds, the grain lines should run straight between the points.

Cut 120 diamonds of blue polka dot fabric and 120 of red polka dot fabric. From the white fabric, cut 120 triangles and 20 squares

To sew your quilt by machine. use mercerized cotton thread and 10 to 12 stitches per inch. To sew by hand, use mercerized cotton thread and sew a running stitch about eight to 10 stitches per inch with a back stitch every two or three inches. Use ¼-inch seam allowances.

continued

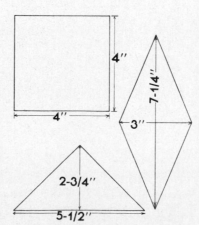

Right: Star-block pattern pieces

Star Pattern Quilt and Pillow Sham *(continued)*

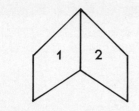

Stitch diamonds together

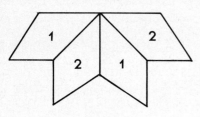

Stitch pairs together

Press all seams to one side, preferably toward the darker color. For instance, press the seams toward the blue or red fabric rather than toward the white fabric.

The construction of this diamond star block requires careful work. If you've never pieced a similar quilt block before, do a little practicing. Use the pattern templates, and cut pieces of scrap fabric. Then assemble a complete practice block from start to finish according to the instructions on the following pages.

For each design block you'll need four blue diamonds, four red diamonds, four white triangles, and four white squares. Separate all your cut pieces into 30 design-block units. You will find it helpful to pin or tack each unit together until you're ready to work on it. See instructions for tacking on pages 6-7.

You may want to piece the star blocks before you cut the separating strips and blocks. Or you may want to do all the cutting at one time. In that case, you'll find cutting diagrams and information on page 42.

Assembling the Blocks

Make the stars first. Begin by sewing a red (1) and blue (2) diamond together (see top left diagram). Sew from one end to the other. Open the diamonds and press the seam allowances flat toward the dark (blue) side. Make three more diamond pairs combining one red and one blue section. As you stitch, always have the same color diamond on top, so you establish a definite right and left side of the unit, keeping the same color on the same side each time. Any deviation from this sequence will destroy the alternating diamond pattern of the finished star.

Next, sew two diamond pairs together as shown in the bottom drawing at the left. Make sure the colors are alternating. When these two diamond pairs are sewn together, you will have completed half the star. Sew two more diamond pairs together to make the second half of the star. Press seams. With right sides together, sew the two halves of the star together along the long straight edge. You should now have one complete eight-pointed star. Open the long seam and press it flat.

Insert the white triangles and squares next, when the star is completely assembled. This step requires patience, accuracy, and a little practice on spare scraps of fabric if you've never done it before. When you set your squares and triangles into the diamond star, remember you are joining pieces cut on the bias (the diamonds) with pieces cut on the straight grain of the fabric (the squares and short sides of the triangles). Because the bias diamond sides tend to stretch more than the sides cut on the straight grain, be extra careful with your piecing at this point. After setting the squares and triangles, you'll find that a good pressing will take care of any minor stretching or puckering problems.

To insert squares into the diamond star, mark one corner of each square with a dot (A) showing where the seams will meet (¼-inch in from two sides). See the top drawing on page 41. On the right side of the fabric, mark the diamond star ¼-inch in from the V on the seam line (B). See the second drawing from the top, on page 41. Use a white or yellow pencil for best results.

With the right sides of a white square and one diamond together, place the dot of the square (dot side up) on top of the dot of the diamond (A on top of B). It will help to stick a straight pin through the two dots to get them accurately lined up. Be sure the edges are straight. When the two points are correctly aligned the diamond point will extend beyond the edge of the square slightly.

With the square on top, sew from the end of the diamond to dot A. Stop with the needle in the fabric. (See drawing third from top). Lift up the presser foot, leaving the needle in place. Rotate the diamond so the V and dot A are directly in front of you. Now, carefully lift up the white square and, with sharp scissors, clip from the edge of the diamond to the needle—but no further. This will ease the fabric so you can turn it, lay it flat, and stitch again.

Follow the bottom drawing and rotate the square on the needle so that the square side C-D lines up with the diamond side E. Pin in place. Put down your presser foot and continue sewing to the outer edge. Practice this technique once or twice and you'll see how simple it is to get pucker-free corners. Piece the other white squares and triangles into the diamond star using the same method. Be careful to place the squares and triangles in the correct position. Turn seams back toward the star and press down. Make 30 star blocks following these instructions. Then, if you haven't already cut the separating strips, now's the time to do it.

Piecing the Quilt Top

Cut and sew separating strips first. Straighten and press the fabric. From the red fabric, cut two border strips (A) 2x87 inches; two border strips (B) 2x103 inches; 14 strips (C) 1¾x106 inches; and 16 strips (D) 1¾x11¾ inches. From white fabric, cut two border strips (E) 2x87 inches; two strips (F) 2x103 inches; five strips (G) 2¼x106 inches; and eight strips (H) 2¼x11¾ inches. From the blue and white polka dot fabric, cut 42 4¾-inch squares. Mark cutting lines on the red and white fabrics with a pencil as shown in the diagrams on the following page. Use a yardstick to help you measure and draw straight lines. Cut the strips carefully along the marked lines.

With right sides together, sew two red lattice strips (C) to either side of one white lattice strip (G). Press. Sew six more (total seven) long strips like this. Now, cut one of these long strips into nine lattice-strip units, each 11¾-inches long. Repeat with the remaining long strips, giving you a total of 63 lattice-strip units.

Sew two short red strips (D) to either side of one short white strip (H). Sew a total of eight lattice-strip units like this. You now have a total of 71 lattice-strip units for your quilt top.

Assemble long separating strips by grouping six blue-dot squares and five lattice-strip units. Sew a blue-dot square to one end of a lattice-strip unit, add another square, then another lattice-strip unit, and so forth, as shown in the "Strip A" drawing on the following page. Press all seams toward the polka dot squares. Make six more long strips like this for a total of seven. Set these strips aside while you assemble the rows of blocks.

Assemble each row of blocks with six lattice-strip units and five star-design blocks. Sew a strip unit to one side of a star block, then sew another strip unit to the opposite side. Continue building up as shown in the "Strip B" diagram on page 42. Press all seams toward the red strips. Make five more long strips like this for a total of six.

continued

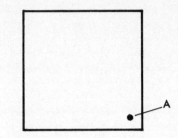

Mark the square

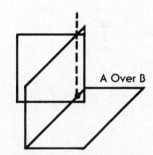

Mark the star

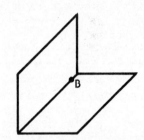

A Over B

Match dots on square and star

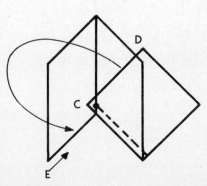

Rotate the square

Star Pattern Quilt and Sham *(continued)*

Cutting Diagram for Red and White Fabric

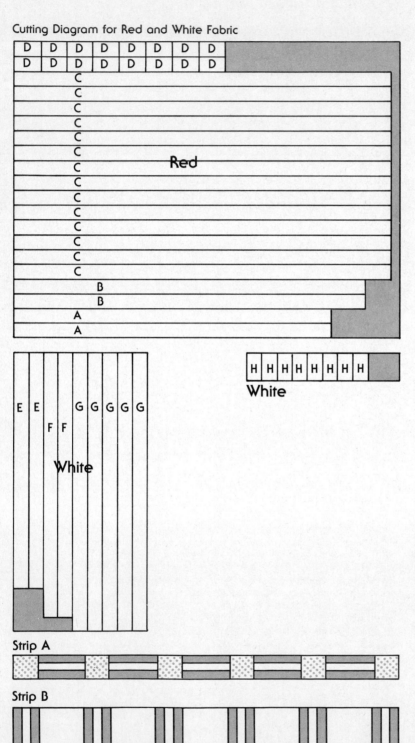

Red

White

White

Strip A

Strip B

Join the rows by sewing a long strip A to the top of a long strip B. Then sew a long strip A to the lower edge of strip B, and continue, alternating A and B strips as shown in the illustration opposite. Be careful to pin the points where strip units and blue squares meet before you sew the long strips together.

Sew shorter white border strips (E) to the bottom and top of the quilt. Sew the longer white border strips (F) to the sides of the quilt. Trim if necessary. Sew the shorter red border strips (A) to the top and bottom of the quilt and the longer border strips (B) to the sides. Trim if necessary. Press all seams back away from the white border strip and toward the dark colors.

Assembling the Quilt

You're now ready to fill the quilt. For a traditional quilted effect, use one layer of high quality polyester quilt batting. For a puffier, comforter effect, use two or three layers of batting.

To create backing for your quilt, cut the six yards of fabric into two three-yard lengths. Sew them together vertically. Press seams.

For a finished edge, place pressed patchwork on top of the batting, right side up. Trim the batting to match your patchwork quilt top. Next, place the backing on top of the patchwork, wrong side up. (Right sides of the patchwork top and the quilt backing are now facing each other.) Trim the backing to match the top and batting, if necessary. Baste all three layers together around the edges, using long running stitches. Baste several rows vertically and horizontally to prevent shifting. Or baste from top to bottom, side to side, and diagonally from corner to corner. Stitch and loosen the machine tension. The fabric side should be on top and the batting underneath as you sew. It's helpful to have a card table or similar support to your left on which to rest the quilt so its weight doesn't pull on the seam while you sew.

Trim the corners of the quilt and excess batting if necessary. Remove basting stitches and turn the quilt right side out through the opening on one side. Straighten corners after the quilt is turned, but don't use a pointed object. Instead, use the eraser end of a pencil. Slip-stitch the opening closed by hand.

Place the quilt on the floor, and straighten the fabric with your hands. Pin all layers together in the center of each block and along the wide borders.

To tie your quilt, secure the three layers with a double thickness of floss (12 strands) and make a tie at least every four inches. In this design, it's best to tie at the end of each point in the star, in the middle of each star, and at the four corners of each design block. For tying instructions, see pages 48-49.

If you prefer quilting to tying, see instructions beginning on page 46. Choose a quilting pattern to hand- or machine-stitch. This particular design could be machine quilted easily and effectively by stitching along the horizontal and vertical lines of the pieced quilt top.

Star-patterned Sham

Cut four small blue polka dot diamonds, four red polka dot diamonds, four white triangles, and four squares for each sham.

Follow the instructions given on page 40 to complete the star block. It's made in the same way as the block for the quilt.

Cut and sew the border strips next. Start by straightening and pressing the fabric. Mark cutting lines with a pencil, using a yard-

stick to help you measure and draw straight lines.

From the red fabric, carefully cut two pieces 2x12 inches and two pieces 3x15 inches. From white fabric, cut two pieces 2x16 inches and two pieces 3x18 inches. Using the blue polka dot fabric, cut two pieces 2x21 inches and two pieces 3x31 inches.

With right sides together, sew the shorter red strips to the top and bottom of the star block. The seam allowance is ¼ inch. Trim excess. Sew longer red strips to the sides. Press. In the same way sew the white strips to the top

and bottom, then to the sides. Finish the border by sewing on the blue dot strips, using the same procedure. Press completely.

For the pillow backing, cut one piece 10½x26½ inches and one piece 13½x26½ inches. Turn under ¼-inch hem on a long side of each piece. First pin narrower piece of backing to pillow top, right sides together. Next, pin on the larger piece. Wider pieces will overlap the narrower pieces slightly. Stitch around all four sides. Clip corners, and reverse pillow sham through the opening in the back. Press.

Traditional—
American
Quilts
and
Quilting

Patchwork quilts are truly one of the most expressive forms of American folk art, as the vintage, one-of-a-kind Log Cabin quilt displayed here so beautifully demonstrates. Log Cabin, with its strip-pieced blocks, is just one of the many quilt patterns that have been handed down to us over the years. Like many others, it has changed with the times, and on pages 52-53 you'll find an exciting contemporary version of this classic pattern. In this section of **Patchwork and Quilting**, you can begin your love affair with the American patchwork quilt. On the following pages you'll discover quilting basics—the old techniques and the new. Then, you'll find step-by-step how-to instructions for treasured American patterns like Windmill, Storm at Sea, and the ever-popular Star of Bethlehem.

Quilting Basics

It's what you do with your quilt after you've pieced or appliquéd the top that makes it a work of art—and a potential heirloom. Whether you're going to stage a neighborhood quilting bee or go it alone with your quilt and a sewing machine, here's a step-by-step guide to what you should know about quilting.

Quilting Patterns

Once your quilt top is completed, the next step is choosing a quilting design that will enhance the patchwork or appliqué of the top. For a pleasing appearance, it's important that the quilting design is compatible with the design of the quilt top. To make sure, draw a portion of your quilting design on tracing paper, or any other transparent paper, and lay it on top of the quilt. Study it and make sure the quilting stitches will augment rather than detract from the beauty of the quilt.

There are three common ways of quilting, and a variety of designs are available as patterns from craft and quilting shops. Or you can design your own quilting pattern.

Outline quilting is probably the most popular form of quilting. Here, the pieced patchwork is delineated by running stitches taken ⅛ to ¼ inch on either side of the seam lines, so each patch is outlined. This not only secures the layers of the quilt to each other, but also gives your quilt a dimensional quality.

In diagonal quilting, another popular pattern, diagonal lines are stitched at regularly spaced intervals across a quilt top. Stitching in the opposite direction results in a diamond quilting pattern.

Quilting in a curved line or scallop is also common. This is often called a shell pattern.

Transferring Your Pattern

No matter which quilting pattern you use, you'll find the following guidelines helpful when transferring it to your quilt top.

A mark that's too dark or indelible can detract from the beauty of the quilt, yet a line that's too light is difficult to stitch. To avoid these pitfalls, use dressmaker's chalk or a chalk pencil. If you use a soft lead pencil, make a dotted rather than a solid line, and cover the dots with your stitches.

Masking tape, in any width you choose, is also handy for marking straight lines. Stick the tape down and stitch slightly beyond both edges. Do not leave the tape on for any length of time, however, or it will make your quilt top gummy. And don't substitute adhesive or cellophane tape.

A template is essential for marking quilting lines for a scalloped or shell pattern. To make one, trace a row of half-circles of the desired size on a strip of cardboard. Then, cut them out along the traced line. Lay the pattern flat on the quilt top and mark the first row along the scalloped edge. To mark the second row, position the scallops so the low point on the curves of the second row is over the high point of the curves in the first row. Mark this row. Continue, alternating the position of the scallops, until the area to be quilted is filled.

A pan lid or plate also makes a good template for a scallop. Attach small pieces of masking tape to the sides of the lid or plate to mark where the area to be traced, and in the middle of the curve to help mark alternate rows of scallops.

Designs traced on paper can be transferred with dressmaker's carbon and a tracing wheel, or by punching holes along the lines with a sharp pencil. Test the washability of carbon before using it.

To make a perforated pattern, trace the pattern onto brown wrapping paper. Then, with the sewing machine unthreaded, stitch along the lines. Lay the pattern on the quilt and mark the fabric by rubbing stamping powder or paste through the holes.

Combining Patterns

When choosing a quilting pattern, keep in mind that several different patterns often look great when combined in one quilt. Sometimes the pieced blocks are quilted along the seam lines; the plain blocks are quilted with a stitched design, such as a wreath or star; and the border is worked in diamonds or scallops.

Assembling the Quilt

When your quilt top is finished and marked for quilting, assemble the materials you need to put the quilt together: the quilt top (pressed and wrinkle free), the backing, the quilt batting, and pins or needle and thread.

For the back of your quilt, select a fabric of the same type and weight as the top. Often you can use a sheet. Or join together the number of lengths of fabric necessary to achieve the proper width. Backing may be plain white or neutral; however, you may also use prints or colors if they coordinate with the quilt top. You may use matching or contrasting fabric to bind the edges of the quilt.

Several types of quilt batting are available. Cotton batting is relatively flat and easy to stitch through when hand quilting. Polyester batting is thicker and makes a puffier quilt. Use several layers of polyester batting for the extra puffy, comforter look. For quilting small items, such as hot pads or place mats, you can also use polyester fleece —a firm, flat but soft padding used in tailoring.

Lay the backing on the floor, face down, and smooth it out until it is perfectly flat. Be sure the grain is straight and the corners square. Then place the batting on top of the backing and smooth it out until there are no wrinkles or lumps.

If you plan to quilt without a quilting frame, pin the batting and backing together and baste. (This gives added stability to the interlining and keeps it from shifting while you quilt.) If you plan to use a quilting frame, skip this step.

Place the pressed and marked quilt top over the batting. Smooth it out and square the corners. Pin through all three layers, starting in the center and going in all directions. Space pins about eight inches apart. Be sure to smooth out any lumps and wrinkles ahead of you as you go along, and take long (one inch), even stitches.

Baste the three layers together (see sketch at right). Using a running stitch, baste on the lengthwise and crosswise grain through the center of the quilt. Then baste diagonally from corner to corner and around the outside edges of the quilt.

Hand Quilting

Hand quilting can be done on a floor frame, on a quilting hoop, or on your lap without a hoop.

A floor frame is essential if quilting is to be a social function, for it allows several people to work on the quilt at the same time. This type of frame consists of two long poles to which the quilt is attached and stretched between the two side braces. The frame is supported by a table-height stand.

To use a floor frame, attach the quilt to the poles and roll it to one side, until the exposed area is tightly stretched. Make sure corners are square. Begin quilting about 12 inches from the edge and quilt toward yourself. When you complete the quilting in one area, roll the quilt under and expose a section of the unstitched top. Stretch the new area tight before quilting.

continued

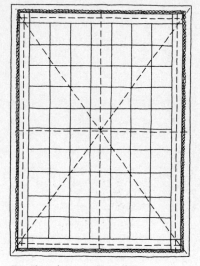

Basting layers together

Quilting Basics *(continued)*

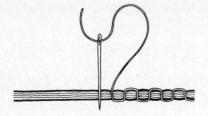

Two-hand quilting stitches

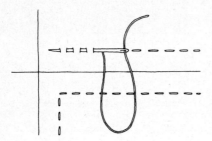

One-hand quilting stitches

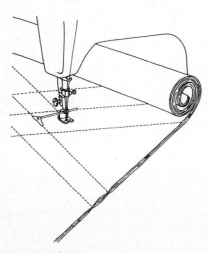

Machine quilting

The quilting hoop resembles an embroidery hoop, but is somewhat larger. It's used in the same way, however; the inner hoop fits under the quilt and the outer hoop on top, holding it tight. Thumbscrews on the hoops adjust to accommodate any thickness of quilt.

When using a hoop, start quilting in the center of the quilt and work toward the edges. As you complete a section, release the hoop and move it to an unstitched area.

Lap quilting requires no equipment. As in quilting with a hoop, you should start at the center of the quilt and work toward the edges. Hold the quilt firmly to keep layers from slipping.

Use waxed quilting thread for hand stitching and either a #8 or #9 sharp needle. Work with a single thread, about 20 inches long. Make sure the thread you choose is similar in color to the quilt fabric. Light-colored quilts usually are stitched in white; dark-colored quilts in blue, brown, or black.

Make short, even stitches. The secret of good quilting is to make sure each stitch goes through all three layers of the quilt. A dull or rough needle will make stitching difficult, so discard blunted needles. A thimble is often helpful when piercing the three layers of a quilt.

Start quilting by knotting the end of the thread and bringing the needle up through all layers of the quilt. Pull the knot through the backing until it's concealed in the batting.

There are two common methods of making a quilting stitch. With a little experimentation, you'll find the one that's most comfortable for you.

One method employs the left hand above the quilt and the right hand below it. Push the needle down through all thick-

nesses with the left hand, then push it up with the right hand, very close to the first stitch. The stitches should be the same length on both sides. (See the top drawing at left.) If you're left-handed, work with the left hand below the quilt and the right hand above it.

The other method is to take two or three running stitches at a time before pulling the thread through. (See the middle drawing at the left.)

When all the quilting is done, release the quilt from the frame and remove the basting threads. Be careful not to pull out any of the quilting stitches.

Machine Quilting

You can machine-quilt most quilting patterns, provided they are not extremely intricate. If you choose to machine-quilt, do the entire quilt with this method. Do not combine machine- and hand-quilting in the same quilt.

To machine-quilt, assemble the backing, batting, and top the same as for hand-quilting. However, you'll need additional basting to machine-quilt. (This helps keep the layers from slipping under the needle on the machine.) Baste horizontal and vertical rows, about four inches apart, over the entire quilt using a fairly short basting stitch.

A quilting foot, while not essential, simplifies the stitching of straight patterns. Place the space bar of the quilting foot to either the right or left of the needle to ensure uniformly spaced lines in the quilting design (see the bottom drawing on the left).

If you're using a portable sewing machine, set it on a large table to support the quilt and keep it off the floor. Extend cabinet models by placing card tables adjacent to the machine.

Use regular mercerized sew-

ing thread and set the machine at six to eight stitches per inch. Loosen the tension and pressure a bit and make a quilt sample with top, batting, and back layers to test stitch tension. Upper and lower threads should lock in the middle of the layers.

Roll the quilt crosswise to the center and place the roll under the arm of the sewing machine. Work, row by row, from the center to the edge. Don't pull the quilt. Guide it gently and stitch at a slow, even pace.

When you've stitched half the quilt, remove it from the machine, roll the completed area, and unroll the unquilted portion. Again, slide the rolled half under the arm of the machine and quilt from the center toward the edge. When you're finished, remove the basting stitches.

Tying Your Quilt

This is a faster means of securing the three layers of a quilt together than quilting; however, it's not as decorative. If producing a work of fabric art is your goal, you will probably want to quilt the finished top. This usually takes anywhere from a couple of weeks to several months. But if time is limited, you may want to speed the process by tying your quilt, which you can do in an afternoon.

To tie a quilt, assemble as for quilting, with the backing, batting, and top laid out smooth and wrinkle-free. Pin and baste the layers together just as you would for quilting. Then place the quilt in a quilting frame if you have one, or work the quilt on the dining room table.

Mark the quilt at three- to eight-inch intervals, across and down. If the quilt is made of blocks, you can tailor your tying to the design and tie at the ends of star points, or at the four corners and center of a block.

Use an embroidery needle and string, yarn, or embroidery floss that either matches or contrasts with the quilt top. Use a single or double strand, depending on the desired effect.

Start at the center of the quilt and work to the edges. Push the needle through the layers and out the back, then reenter from the back, going through the layers and coming up ⅛ inch from the point of entry. Allow two inches of thread at either end of the stitch and cut. Tie the threads in a square knot and then trim the ends.

If you don't want the ties to show on the front of the quilt, reverse the procedure and tie the threads on the back side.

Finishing Your Quilt

There are a number of ways to finish the edges of the quilt. You can make borders by using bias tape or the same fabric you used for the quilt top, or by bringing the backing fabric around the edge to the front to form the binding. Or you can skip the binding altogether and stitch the top of your quilt to the back.

Finishing the edges without binding is possible on quilts with bands of fabric bordering a central design. The borders themselves enclose the design in the same way that an applied band or bias tape does. So you can sew the quilt top to the backing and batting without a separate binding strip. Use this method only when tying a quilt.

To finish a quilt this way, make sure the batting and backing are basted together firmly. Then lay the batting and backing down on the floor, with the right side of the backing fabric up and smooth out all wrinkles. Lay the right side of the quilt top down on the backing fabric, and pin all the way around.

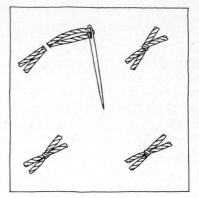

Tying the quilt

continued

Quilting Basics *(continued)*

French binding

Machine-stitch around all four sides, leaving a section of one side open for turning the quilt. Turn the quilt through the opening and push out the corners, using the eraser end of a pencil. Slip-stitch the opening closed.

If you're using a commercial bias tape, pin the tape to the quilt top, right sides together, starting in the middle of a side. Then sew around all the edges of the quilt to secure the tape. Using the sewing machine will give you a stronger stitch, but be careful to keep the corners neat and square. Trim away the excess fabric and fold the tape to the back. Pin the tape in place and blindstitch by hand.

To make fabric binding, cut strips two inches wide and join them into a strip long enough to go completely around the quilt. Cut either with the grain or on the bias. If the quilt edge is scalloped or shaped, cut the binding on the bias. Attach the same way as bias tape.

To make bias binding, cut strips at a 45-degree angle across the grain of the fabric. To find the bias, fold the lower edge of the fabric up along the selvage edge. With your thumb, press the fold gently to form a light crease. Using this crease as a guide, cut strips twice the width of the finished binding, plus ¼ inch for each seam allowance.

To join lengths of bias, put the short ends of two strips together, right sides facing, and stitch with the grain (not the bias) in a ¼-inch seam. The seam will look diagonal on the binding. Tack both ends of the seam with a backstitch. Open up the seam and press it flat.

If you're buying bias binding, you may have to join several packages together. If you do, use the joining method given above to reach the proper length.

French binding is a means of finishing off your quilt edges with bias binding when durability and strength are important. To use this method, cut the bias strips four times as wide as the finished width, plus ¼ inch for each seam allowance. Fold the strips in half lengthwise, with wrong sides together, and press down. This will give you a double bias strip with two raw edges on one side and a fold on the other. Apply this double binding the same as regular bias binding. Be sure the two raw edges of the bias strip are placed next to the raw edge of the quilt. Stitch the binding down securely, then turn the folded edge to the reverse side of the quilt and stitch it down with a blindstitch. (See drawing at left.)

The backing fabric can also be used to bind the raw edges. When backing is used, the band is usually rather narrow — ½ to two inches wide. If you plan to bind the edges this way, make allowances for the band when you're assembling the quilt for quilting. The backing fabric will have to be larger than the quilt top and batting. Plan for the backing to extend beyond the quilt top by double the width of the band, plus ½ inch to turn under as a seam allowance.

Extend the batting beyond the quilt top to the width of the finished band, less ¼ inch. For example, if you want a two-inch band, extend the backing 4½ inches beyond the quilt top, and trim the batting to extend 1¾ inches beyond the top. Since the three layers are staggered in size, plan to pin the margin of the backing over the batting to protect it during the quilting process. After quilting, remove all the pins and lay the quilt out flat.

Following the drawings at the right, fold the raw edges of the backing forward ½ inch all the way around the quilt. Press down lightly. Measuring in ½ inch diagonally, clip off the point of each corner. (See the drawing at top left.)

Next fold the corner of the backing over the batting, but do not fold the batting itself. Pin the corner to the quilt top, ¼ inch from the edge. (See drawing at center left.) Press.

Fold the sides of the backing over the batting. Place the folded edge of the backing ¼ inch in from the edge of the quilt top. The corners miter themselves. (See drawing at lower left.)

Baste this band down all around the quilt. Machine- or hand-sew ⅛ inch from the folded edge. Pivot at the corners. Slip-stitch the mitered corner.

You can use this same method of binding with the front of the quilt (the quilt top) overlapping the backing. Just reverse the procedure outlined above.

Adding Ruffles and Flounces

Ruffles and flounces also are used to edge quilts, particularly those with appliquéd and tied tops. The method of application is the same for both, the difference between them being that a flounce is deeper than a ruffle and often extends to the floor.

To add a ruffle to your quilting project, first measure all four sides. Plan to ruffle a strip of fabric twice this length. Next determine how wide you want your ruffle and cut fabric strips twice this width adding ½ inch for seam allowances. Join the strips together to form one long strip. Then join the two ends of the strip to form a circle.

Next, fold this strip in half lengthwise with the right side of the fabric out. Press down. Using a long gathering stitch on the machine, sew two lines of stitching ¼ to ½ inch in from the raw edges. Carefully pull the bobbin threads to create the ruffle. Gather a small section at a time to make sure the ruffling isn't too tight or too loose. For instance, mark off a 36-inch section with pins, then gather it until it measures 18 inches. That way, you will know your ruffle will come close to fitting around your quilt with only minor adjustments.

When the ruffle is gathered, start pinning it to the quilt top. Place the ruffle on top of the quilt face, with the raw edges of the quilt and the ruffle even. Baste the ruffle in place. Machine-stitch ¼ inch in from the raw edges.

To join the quilt top to the back and batting, lay the back down on the floor, wrong side up, and place the batting over it. Pin and baste the batting to the quilt backing, following the instructions on page 47. When the two layers are secured, turn them over so the batting is on the floor and the right side of the backing fabric is up. Carefully place the quilt top and ruffle on top of the backing fabric, right sides together. Make sure the ruffle is tucked inside and smoothed out so its bottom edge won't get caught in the seam. Pin all layers and baste.

Machine-stitch all around the edges of the quilt, leaving an opening on one side for turning the quilt. Sew with the quilt top up so you can see the stitching line securing the ruffle to the top. Be sure you sew inside this seam; otherwise, it will show when the quilt is turned.

Turn the quilt through the opening and straighten the corners, using the eraser end of a pencil. Slip-stitch the opening closed. Smooth the quilt out and tie to hold the three layers together. Remove all basting and gathering threads.

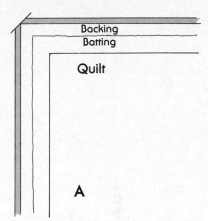

Turning under backing seam allowance

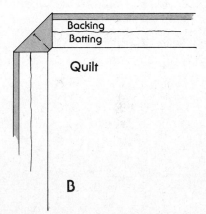

Folding corner over batting

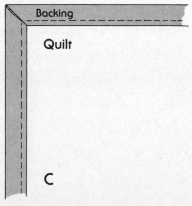

Folding band over batting and stitching to quilt top

New-fashioned Log Cabin Quilt

A traditional Log Cabin quilt, like the one shown on pages 44-45, is made of increasingly longer rectangles pieced together, L-shaped fashion, to form a block. But today, even the Log Cabin has gone prefab. This updated version of the famous quilt is made of strips of fabric sewn together diagonally across a square. When the squares are put together, they create the Log Cabin look.

Materials
Assorted colored fabric for
  strips
2¾ yards 45-inch-wide white
  fabric for center strips
6 yards 45-inch-wide medium
  blue fabric for backing
Quilt batting

Directions
The placement diagram below contains four blocks of this contemporary Log Cabin quilt. Enlarge ¼ of the diagram (1 block), and then make templates of the pattern pieces. Cut the center strip in each block from white fabric, or from some other light or bright color of your choice. (It's the consistent color of the center strip that creates the square effect in the quilt top.) Cut remaining strips from fabric in assorted colors and patterns. Be sure to add ¼-inch seam allowances to all sides of the pieces.

Sew the strips in each block together. For a full-size quilt, make 90 blocks. If you're making a larger or smaller quilt, adjust the number of blocks. Press all the seams flat.

When all the blocks are completed, lay them out on the floor and arrange them in a pleasant color pattern according to the placement diagram. You'll need nine rows of 10 blocks each. Be sure to position the blocks so the direction of the strips alternates, forming diamond shapes with the white center strips. Sew all the blocks in each row together. Then sew the rows together and press open the seams.

The edges of this quilt are bound by a border of backing fabric turned over the quilt top. See instructions on page 50 for assembling a quilt in this manner. (General directions for either hand or machine quilting begin on page 47.) The quilt shown here is hand-stitched around each square and on each side of the center strip.

Log Cabin

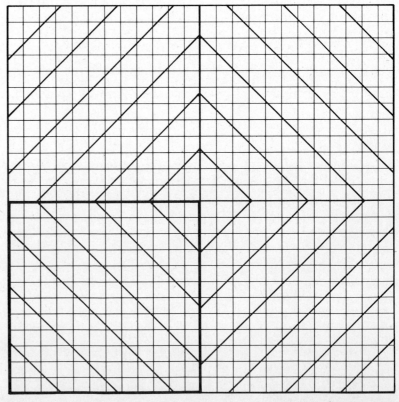

1 Square=3/4 Inch

Classic Star of Bethlehem Quilt

At left is a simplified version of the exquisite and inspirational Star of Bethlehem quilt, opposite.

Materials

7¾ yards 45-inch-wide yellow
   fabric
1¼ yards 45-inch-wide green
   fabric
1½ yards 45-inch-wide print
   fabric
1 sheet of 8½ yards fabric
   for backing
Quilt batting

Star-point assembly diagram

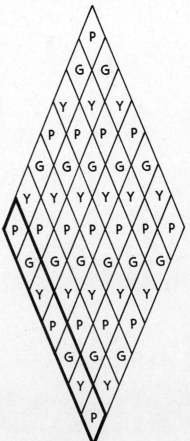

Directions

For a 94-inch-diameter star, first make a diamond pattern by drawing a line 6¾ inches long. Bisect this line at the midpoint with a second line 2¹³⁄₁₆ inches long drawn at right angles to the first line. Connect the end points of these two lines to make a diamond whose sides are each 3⅝ inches long. Cut 136 print diamonds (P), 128 green (G), and 128 yellow (Y). Cut four yellow triangles 37x26¼x26¼ inches and four yellow 26¼-inch squares. Add ¼-inch seam allowances to all pieces. Following the diagram at right, sew diamonds into rows, then join rows into a large, diamond-shaped section. Make eight sections, and piece them together into an eight-pointed star.

Stitch large yellow squares and triangles in place. Next cut and sew 4-inch-wide strips of print fabric to the top and bottom edges of the quilt top. Then cut two 3-inch-wide green strips and sew one to each of the print strips. Cut two 4-inch-wide yellow strips and sew them to the green strips. Next cut and sew a 1½-inch-wide print strip to each of the side edges. Cut two 4-inch-wide yellow strips and sew one to each of the side print strips. Press seams open.

Assemble the quilt according to the general instructions beginning on page 46. Quilt along the seams joining the small diamonds, and extend the stitching across the large squares and triangles. To finish, turn excess top fabric to back in a band.

Lone Star Quilt

Here's another interpretation of the Star of Bethlehem or single-star quilt–this time pieced from smaller diamond shapes. The diamond pattern is approximately 72 inches in diameter.

Materials

Assorted print and solid fabrics in light and dark shades (see directions)

4 yards plain light-colored fabric for squares and tri-angles

1 sheet or 5½ yards fabric for backing

Quilt batting

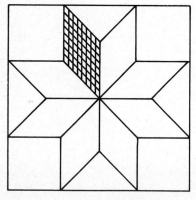

Above: Placement diagram for quilt

Right: Placement diagram for star-point

Directions

To make the diamond pattern for this quilt, mark a line 4½ inches long and bisect it at right angles with a line 1⅞ inches long. Connect the ends with diagonal lines 2⁷⁄₁₆ inches long. Add ¼-inch seam allowances.

If you study the photograph shown opposite, you'll see that the center of the star is made of dark fabric. Diamonds in the next five rows of the star are in lighter shades of fabric, followed by two rows of darker print fabrics. Note that the same fabric is used for each diamond piece in any given row for the first eight rounds of diamonds (the center part of the star pattern). Then, as the star separates into its points, more variety is used in the fabrics for each row of dia-monds, but the color value (light or dark) is the same for the cor-responding row in each point. Thus, the beauty of this design lies in the consistency of the fabrics used for the inner portion of the pattern and the consistency of the *intensity* of the colors in the arms of the star—even though the same fabrics are not used throughout.

To help you in planning your quilt, the placement diagram for one star-point (below) is keyed for light (L) and dark (D) shades. The numbers indicate how many small diamonds you'll need to cut from the same fabric for the inside portion of the star. You can cut about 15 diamonds across a 5x45-inch piece of fabric.

Follow the general instructions given on page 55 for sewing your quilt. When the eight sections are completed and sewn together, lay the star out on the floor. Measure the lengths of the points to deter-mine how large to cut the squares for the corners and the triangles to go between the points. Add seam allowances, and then cut and sew these pieces in place. Your star pattern should now measure about 72 inches square.

Since a full-size quilt is usually about 80x90 inches, you'll need to add about nine inches of fabric to each end of the star and then about four inches of fabric at each side. The fabric can be a single strip or several strips of the same or varying widths. Be sure to add seam allowances when you cut the strips.

When your quilt top is completely finished, assemble the entire quilt, following instructions beginning on page 46. Machine- or hand-quilt along the seams that join the small diamonds and let the stitching lines extend out onto the squares and triangles. Finish the edges by bringing the backing fabric to the front in a band, or by binding them with a fabric used in the quilt top.

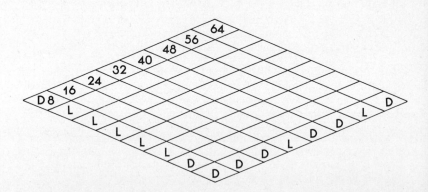

Storm at Sea Quilt

Diamonds, squares, and triangles are all rigid geometric shapes, yet by piecing them together in the intricate pattern diagramed below, you can create the curves and rhythms of waves. Storm at Sea is one of the oldest and most popular patchwork patterns in America, and a real test of the quilter's piecing skill.

Materials

Light blue, dark blue, and white
fabric totaling approximately
7 yards
5¾ yards blue backing fabric
Quilt batting

Color Key
A, C, F = Light Blue
B, E, G = White
D, H = Dark Blue

Directions

Enlarge the diagram below and make templates of cardboard or sandpaper for each of the different shapes.

For a 76x88-inch quilt, cut sufficient pieces, in the appropriate colors, to make up 42 large squares (pattern pieces A, B, C), 97 rectangles (pieces D, E), and 56 small squares (pieces F, G, H). Be sure to add ¼-inch seam allowances to all the pieces as you cut. First piece all the large squares, the small squares, and the rectangles separately. Press all the seams flat and away from the white areas and toward the dark colors.

When all the units are pieced, sew together into a long strip six large squares and seven rectangles (as in the right two-thirds of the diagram). Start and end with a rectangle. Make seven of these strips.

Then sew together into strips six rectangles and seven small squares (as in the left third of the diagram). Start and end with a small square. Make eight of these strips. Now sew the strips together alternating narrow and wide strips, and starting and ending with a narrow strip. Press the quilt top flat.

Cut and piece the blue backing fabric. Since the raw edges of the quilt will be bound with backing fabric, you'll need to cut the backing larger than the top. Assemble the quilt according to instructions beginning on page 47. Outline-quilt around the shapes in the quilt top. Finally, follow the instructions for making a border of backing fabric on page 50.

Storm At Sea

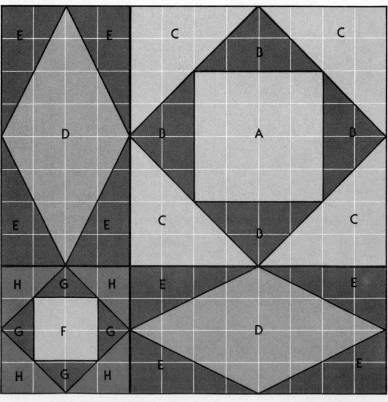

1 Square = 1 Inch

Easy-to-Stitch Windmill Quilt

*Every quilt is a
one-of-a-kind work of art,
deriving its individuality
from the colors and prints
of selected fabrics, as well
as from the quilter's
unique interpretation of a
given design. The quilt
shown here, for instance,
illustrates an ingenious
way of piecing blocks of
the ever-popular windmill
pattern into a most
unusual quilt top.*

*The basic windmill
block is composed of nine
squares. The center
square and four corner
squares of each block are
cut from the same fabric,
while the four slashed
squares (composed of two
triangles each) are cut and
pieced from two
contrasting fabrics,
suggesting the vanes of
the windmill. On some
blocks the vanes are
pieced in one direction,
but in the opposite
direction on others. The
choice of colors and
alternation in piecing
gives the completed quilt
top a pinwheeling sense
of motion.*

Materials

Assorted print, gingham, and
   solid color fabrics for the
   windmill pattern blocks
4 yards 45-inch-wide green
   fabric for background piecing
6 yards 45-inch-wide backing
   fabric
Quilt batting

Directions

The following instructions are for making an 85x102-inch quilt.
Each finished block is 12 inches square. Enlarge the diagram below,
and make templates for the square and triangular pattern pieces.
Next draw a 12-inch square and cut it in half along the diagonal to
make two 12x12x17-inch right-angle triangles. Cut one of these
triangles in half again to make a 12x8½x8½-inch right-angle triangle.
These two triangles (one large and one small) will be your templates
for cutting the green background pieces of the quilt top.

From the assorted print, gingham, and solid fabrics, cut enough
small squares and triangles to make 28 full windmill blocks and four
diagonal half-blocks (for half-blocks, see dotted line on diagram).
From the green fabric, cut 54 large triangles and 12 small triangles.
Remember to add ¼-inch seam allowances to *all* pattern pieces.
Piece blocks according to diagram (remembering to alternate the
direction of the vanes on half the blocks). Next, set blocks together
into strips with triangles between each block, as in the photo. Three
strips of blocks will have five complete windmill blocks, pieced
together with ten large green triangles and four smaller triangles
(two each at either end of the strip). Two rows will have five complete pattern blocks, and a half-block at either end, pieced together
with 12 large green triangles. Sew all five strips together to complete
the top. Assemble the finished quilt top, batting, and backing, and
complete according to quilting instructions on pages 46 through 51.

Windmill

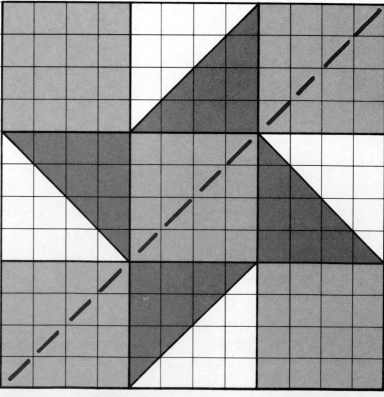

A   B

1 Square=1 Inch

Appliqué-

An Added Dimension

When early quilters wanted to work with more pictorial designs than pieced stars or log cabins, they turned to appliqué. Today's quilters do the same. Appliqué is a needle art form that lets you decorate fabric with shapes you couldn't possibly achieve in patchwork. It's also a stunning complement to pieced work, as the butterflies and blossoms on this page so beautifully demonstrate. Here's an entire section full of eye-appealing appliqué projects—from some easily executed designs to some real works of art (all with instructions, of course). Directions for this appliquéd quilt top are on pages 66-67.

Appliqué Basics

Basting the appliqué

Slip-stitching to fabric

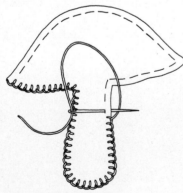

Adding blanket stitch

Appliqué shares honors with patchwork as one of the most popular methods of creating attractive quilt tops. The two crafts have something else in common, too. They're perfect ways to make use of every last scrap of fabric in your sewing basket.

The basic difference is that in patchwork, small pieces of fabric are sewn or pieced together to form designs. In appliqué, bits of fabric are cut into shapes and stitched to a background fabric to create the design. When making a quilt, appliqué can be sewn to blocks which are then joined —or it can be worked over the entire surface area so that no piecing is necessary. Appliqué can be done by hand-stitching, or zigzag stitching on your sewing machine.

Selecting Fabrics

Fabric used for appliqué should be soft but firmly woven. It should not fray easily or stretch out of shape. Some of the most practical fabrics for appliqué are cotton and cotton blends, calico, percale, broadcloth, and muslin. If your appliqué project will be dry-cleaned rather than washed, you may use wools, velvets, and silks for special effects.

Selecting a Design

The first step in any appliqué work is to choose or create the design you want. There are no rules here. Anything you like can be appliquéd, whether your taste runs to traditional flowers or contemporary art. When you've decided on a design, enlarge it to the size you'll want to use on your quilt top. Make a sandpaper or cardboard template for each shape; or if the shapes are to be repeated frequently, make several. Then as the edges of one template become worn from tracing, you can discard it for another.

When appliquéing, always trace your designs on the right side of the fabric.

Hand Appliqué

Hand appliqué designs should be traced on your fabric with at least ½ inch between the marked lines. When designs are marked, machine-stitch all around the edge, following the marked line. Use small straight stitches and thread that matches the fabric. This machine stitch makes it easier to turn under the raw edges, especially along curved areas.

Cut out the design ¼ inch beyond the stitched line. Clip the seam allowance almost to the stitching line along curves, and trim the corners. Fold under the raw edges, rolling the stitching line to the underside.

Place your appliqué pieces on the background fabric. If you're appliquéing blocks for a quilt top, it's important to position the appliqué pieces in each square in exactly the same way. One way is to fold the background square and press the folds in lightly. The creases will act as a guideline or grid for positioning appliqué pieces. Fold the square diagonally from corner to corner forming an "X," or fold the fabric in quarters to create two intersecting lines.

Another method is to make a placement pattern of tracing paper. Position the appliqué pieces as accurately as you can, then lay the tracing paper pattern over the block, check the position of the pieces, and make any adjustments necessary.

When pieces are placed, baste to secure them while you're stitching (see top drawing at left). Never stretch the fabric on an embroidery hoop or frame when working hand appliqué. Thread used for appliqué should match the fabric. Decorative stitches added after pieces are appliquéd may be worked in contrasting thread.

Slip-stitch the piece to the background fabric using a sharp needle and a double length of thread. Anchor the thread in the backing material under the piece to be appliquéd. Then bring it up through the backing and the folded edge of the appliqué piece. Fold the base fabric back so you have two folded edges facing you (the block and the appliqué piece). Then slip one stitch through the appliqué, and the other through the fold in the background fabric. Stitches should be $1/8$ to $1/4$ inch apart (see middle drawing at the left).

A blanket stitch can be added to the outside edge of the appliquéd piece. Use embroidery floss and work from left to right. Bring the needle up at the edge of the appliqué, and hold down thread with the left thumb. Insert the needle a little to the right of the starting point, about $1/8$ to $1/4$ inch from the folded edge. Then bring it out directly below the edge of the appliqué, being sure to go through the base fabric. Draw the needle through the overloop of the thread (see the bottom drawing at the left).

Machine Appliqué

Machine appliqué requires the same kinds of fabric, with designs marked on the right side. Cut out the traced design, allowing at least $1/2$ inch for seams on all sides. Position appliqué pieces on the background fabric and baste in place, just inside the marking line of the design.

Using a short, straight stitch and matching thread, machine-stitch on the marked lines. Then set your machine to a zigzag satin stitch. A narrow satin stitch fits easier into small places, but a wide satin stitch gives appliqué a distinctly outlined look. To get the best results, the tension you

place on the fabric with your hands should be even. Press your fingertips down firmly and guide the fabric carefully. Never pull the work, or stitches will be uneven. Zigzag over the stitched line of the appliqué piece (see drawing at right).

If your design requires stitching a 90-degree angle, zigzag up to the corner and leave the needle in the fabric on the outside line of your stitch. Then lift the presser foot and pivot the fabric. Lower the presser foot and start your stitching so the first stitch goes toward the inside of the design, overlapping the stitch just made, then continue stitching.

To finish, pull the thread to the underside and tie. Using embroidery scissors with sharp points, cut away the excess fabric very close to the stitch line.

If the fabrics you're working are lightweight and tend to draw during machine stitching, place a piece of organdy under the base fabric and trim away the excess after appliquéing (see bottom drawing at the right).

If your machine does not have a zigzag stitch, you can still use it for appliquéing. Prepare the pieces as for hand appliqué, but machine-stitch the piece in place. Use short stitches and work close to the design's edge.

Reverse Appliqué

To create interesting results with reverse appliqué, cut away the design from the top piece of fabric, allowing the background piece to show through. Turn under the raw edges of the top fabric and pin in place. Baste to hold the fabric in position, then, following the directions for slip-stitching, stitch the two pieces of fabric together along the edge of the design. If you choose, add decorative stitches to the slip-stitched edge.

Zigzag stitching

Trimming organdy from back of appliquéd piece.

Appliquéd Butterflies and Blossoms (shown on pages 62-63)

Butterflies and flowers are both popular designs for appliqué, and in this delightful quilt top, they combine in bold, colorful blocks. Although old-style quilts often used these same motifs, their scale and dynamic color give this quilt an exciting modern appearance.

Materials
4 yards muslin
1½ yards orange check,
   45-inch fabric
1½ yards solid orange,
   45-inch fabric
Assorted prints and solids
   for appliqué pieces
1 sheet or 6 yards fabric
   for backing
Polyester batting

Directions
Instructions are for a 64x76-inch quilt.

Enlarge the drawing at right to fit a 13-inch finished block, and make a tracing paper pattern. With carbon paper, trace the outline of each appliqué piece on cardboard and cut out templates. (Note: left and right wings, body, leaves, and flower motif are each cut as single shapes. Details are embroidered on after shapes have been appliquéd in place.) Save the tracing paper pattern to use as a placement guide for the appliqué pieces.

Cut 30 butterflies and 30 blossoms. Bodies of butterflies and leaves of flowers should be cut of dark fabric; butterfly wings and flower petals should be cut from assorted prints and solids. Remember when transferring patterns to your fabric to trace with the fabric right side up and to add ¼-inch seam allowances to all pieces before cutting.

Cut 30 13½-inch squares of muslin, 49 strips of orange checked fabric 3x13½ inches long, and 20 three-inch squares of solid orange. Cut four solid orange strips 3x91 inches long and four strips 3x75 ½ inches long. Piece strips if necessary. Cut eight three-inch squares of orange check. (Measurements for strips and squares include ¼-inch seam allowances.)

Position the leaves on the muslin block using the tracing paper pattern as a guide. Follow general instructions on the preceding pages and appliqué. Place the flower petals over the leaves and appliqué. Position butterfly wings and appliqué, then top them with the body sections. Appliqué. Embroider petal details on the flowers and antennae on butterflies. Add decorative stitches to the appliqué. If you're working by hand, use a buttonhole or blanket stitch on the outer edges of wings and petals, and an outline stitch to separate the flower petals and centers. If machine appliquéing, use a narrow satin stitch. Make 30 appliquéd blocks.

Make rows of blocks by alternating butterfly squares and orange checked strips, starting and ending with blocks. Use five blocks and four checked strips for each row, and be sure that all butterflies are facing the same direction.

Make four joining strips by alternating checked strips and solid squares, starting and ending with checked strips. Use six strips and five squares for each joining strip. Sew one row of blocks to one joining strip, making sure the solid square is positioned directly over the checked strip separating the blocks. Sew another row of blocks to the other side of the joining strip. Continue alternating block rows and joining strips until the quilt top is completed.

Sew one check square to each end of the four 75½-inch-long solid orange strips. Sew one of these border strips to the top of the quilt and one to the bottom. Set the other two aside. Sew one 91-inch-long solid orange border strip to each long side of the quilt. Set the other two strips aside. Sew ends of the long border strips to the checked corner squares, and press all seams in the completed quilt top.

Assemble the quilt top, batting, and backing, and quilt following the instructions starting on page 46. Outline-quilt appliqué pieces and quilt along seams that join blocks and strips.

Join the four remaining border pieces to form a large "frame." Pin frame in place on the face of the completed quilt, right sides together, and sew around all four sides of the quilt. Clip corners, turn, and press. Turn under raw edges and stitch this fabric frame to the backing fabric to finish the quilt.

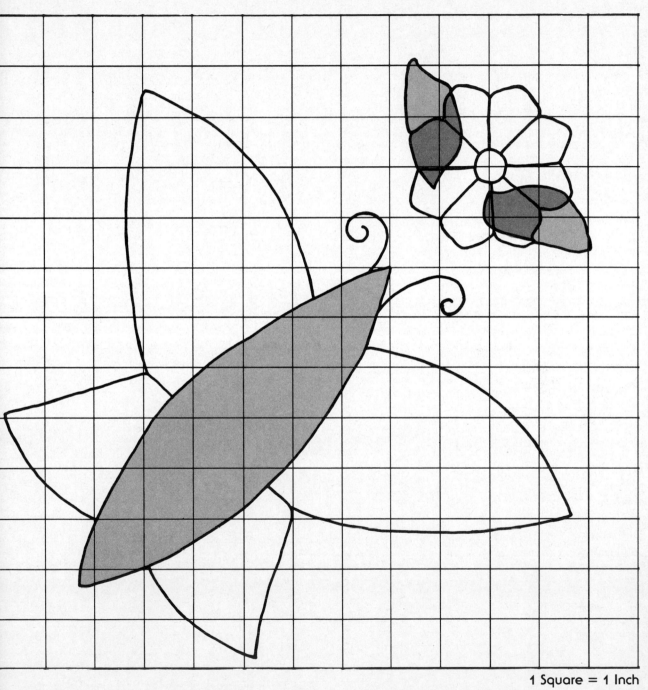

1 Square = 1 Inch

Appliquéd Dresden Plate Quilt Top

One of America's all-time favorite appliqué designs is the Dresden China Plate, also called Aster or Friendship Ring. This intriguing quilt pattern has several variations. For example, here you see both rounded and pointed pieces in the plate, with the center circle of the design slashed and reverse appliquéd to give an interesting "cathedral window" effect. Dresden Plate is often pieced entirely in one printed fabric with a solid center, or in various prints and solids of a single color fabric.

Materials

2¼ yards muslin
1½ yards red fabric
Assorted print fabrics
  for appliqué
5 yards backing fabric and
  one sheet Polyester batting

Directions

Enlarge the pattern below. Cut all pieces with a ¼-inch seam allowance. Cut 15 14½-inch squares of muslin and eight three-inch squares. From print fabric, cut 240 pieces using pattern piece A. From red fabric, cut 60 pieces using pattern B, and 15 circles using pattern C. (Mark dotted inside fold lines on each circle.) Cut 22 strips of red fabric, 14x3 inches. Sew together pieces A and B with four print A pieces between each red B piece. When the pieced circle is completed, center it on a 14½-inch square of muslin and appliqué according to instructions on pages 64 and 65. Place pattern piece C in the center of the pieced circle. Clip and turn under the curved inside edges to reveal a "window" of muslin beneath. Appliqué piece C in place, using black thread and a running stitch. Add a decorative blanket stitch to the outside edge of the appliquéd plate.

Join together three Dresden Plate blocks with red strips separating each block. Make five of these block strips. Next make four joining strips by sewing together one red strip, one muslin square, a second red strip, and another muslin square, ending with a red strip. Sew one strip of blocks to one joining strip, making sure the small muslin squares are positioned over the red strips that separate the blocks. Add a second strip of blocks to the other side of the joining strip, and continue alternating block strips and joining strips until the quilt top is complete. Press seams. Assemble the quilt top, batting, and backing, and quilt according to the directions starting on page 46.

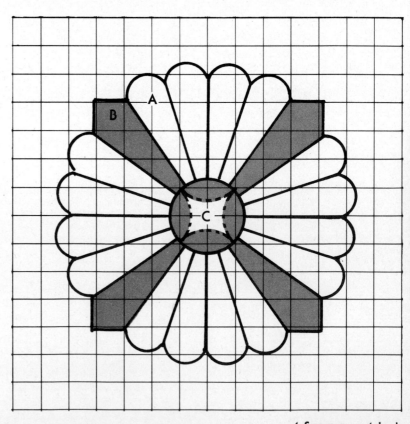

1 Square = 1 Inch

Colorful, Contemporary Butterfly Quilt

If there's a bedroom in your home that needs livening up, nothing will do it faster than this appliquéd quilt, all abloom with butterflies and stylized posies.

Materials

(All fabrics listed are
   44-45 inches wide)
¼ yard yellow
2 yards gold
2 yards orange
1¾ yards rust
1 yard scarlet
¼ yard burgundy
⅛ yard magenta
1½ yards hot pink
6 yards apple green
¼ yard kelly green
⅛ yard white
1 skein white embroidery floss
1 skein burgundy embroidery
   floss
Polyester batting

Directions

The dimensions given here will produce a quilt approximately 67x92 inches, suitable for a twin bed with dust ruffle. Instructions for enlarging the quilt are on page 77, so you can customize your quilt to the size of your bed.

Start by preshrinking and pressing all fabrics. Make the apple green backing sheet first by cutting the six yards of fabric into three equal lengths. These will measure about 72 inches long. Cut a 15-inch-wide strip from the length of one of these so it measures 15x72 inches. Sew this narrow strip between the two other uncut pieces using ½-inch seam allowances. This will give you a 72x103-inch sheet to use as backing for your quilt. Press the seams open. Use the rest of the green fabric for cutting appliqué pieces.

Each quilt block is keyed with a number. Study the block placement diagram on page 72 to familiarize yourself with the sections of the quilt. Colors for each appliqué piece are indicated by the letter symbols given in the color guide on page 76.

Using the graph drawings on pages 73 through 76 as size guides, start by cutting out all the background blocks. Cut blocks 7, 12, 14, 18 and 20 from gold fabric. Cut blocks 1, 8, 10, 15, and 21 from orange. From the rust fabric cut blocks 3, 9, 13, and 17. Use the scarlet fabric for blocks 4, 6, and 19. Cut blocks 2, 5, 11, and 16 from the hot pink fabric.

The dotted line on the drawings indicates the seam line; the solid line is the cutting line. Cut the blocks ¼ inch outside the indicated cutting line to compensate for any drawing-up that occurs while appliquéing the blocks. Excess fabric will be trimmed later.

Enlarge each block to its actual size using tracing paper. With carbon paper, trace the outline of each appliqué piece onto lightweight cardboard or heavy paper. Since each pattern piece will be used only once, making a durable template isn't essential. Keep the tracing paper pattern intact to use as a placement guide.

This quilt is a combination of reverse appliqué and regular appliqué techniques, but if you prefer, the entire quilt may be appliquéd the usual way. The following blocks are worked in regular appliqué: 2, 4, 7, 10, 11, 12, 13, 14, 16, 17, 18, and 19. The following are done in reverse appliqué: 1, 3, 5, 6, 8, 9, 15, 20, and 21.

The diagram in the upper left corner of page 72 shows you how reverse appliqué is done. Instead of sewing a shape to the background fabric, the shape is cut out of the background fabric, leaving a ¼-inch allowance on the inside, to be turned under and sewn to an under-fabric which shows through the cutout shape. The under-fabric has to be cut large enough so that the background fabric can be pinned to it as you sew. The inner details are done afterward in the same way. Because of this, you need not trace inner details of the butterfly when you trace the outer outline on reverse appliqué blocks, since the inner part will be cut out and removed. Trace inner details as each layer is completed. (In both reverse and regular appliqué, the body of each butterfly is appliquéd on top of the wings after the butterfly wings have been appliquéd.) When turning under the edges for reverse appliqué, curved edges and corners should be clipped. Cut only a few inches at a time to help keep the piece in position. It's best to cut a small portion, sew it, then repeat clipping and stitching until the shape is completely appliquéd.

continued

Colorful, Contemporary Butterfly Quilt *(continued)*

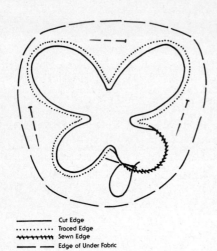

Cut Edge
.... Traced Edge
ʍʍʍʍ Sewn Edge
— — — Edge of Under Fabric

Reverse appliqué technique
(for blocks 1, 3, 5, 6, 8, 9, 15,
20 and 21)

Quilt block placement diagram

1	2	3	
5 / 6 / 7			4
8 / 9 / 10			11 / 12
13 / 14 / 15 / 16			17
18	19	20	21

Pin the appropriate tracing paper patterns to the matching cut fabric backing blocks, centering the appliqué pattern carefully. Use dressmaker's carbon and a tracing wheel to trace just enough marks to indicate the position of the appliqué shapes. If you reverse appliqué the blocks so indicated (see diagram, above left), trace the entire appliqué outline on the blocks rather than just placement markings.

Next, working one block at a time, trace the appliqué shapes onto the appropriate color fabrics. (Refer to the color symbol key on page 76.) Trace around each appliqué piece on the right side of the fabric and cut out leaving a ¼-inch seam allowance on all edges. This will be clipped and turned under in the appliquéing.

continued

1 Square=1 Inch

Colorful, Contemporary Butterfly Quilt *(continued)*

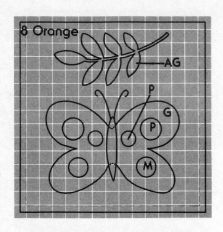

1 Square = 1 Inch

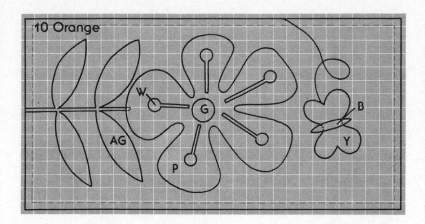

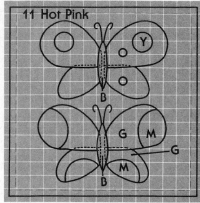

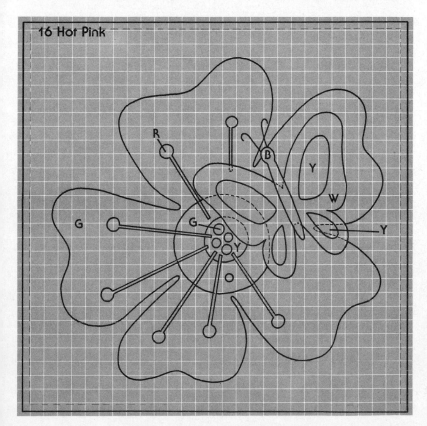

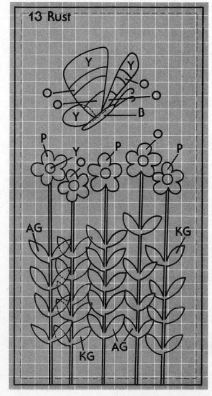

1 Square=1 Inch

continued

Colorful, Contemporary Butterfly Quilt *(continued)*

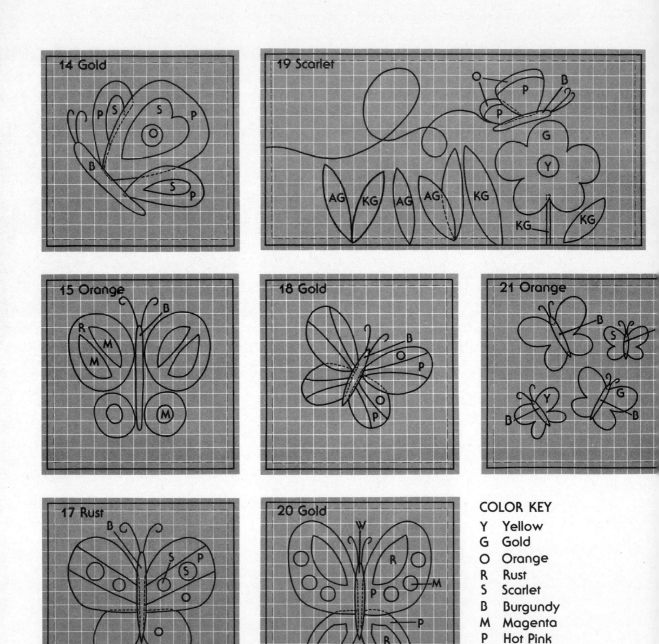

14 Gold

19 Scarlet

15 Orange

18 Gold

21 Orange

17 Rust

20 Gold

COLOR KEY

Y   Yellow
G   Gold
O   Orange
R   Rust
S   Scarlet
B   Burgundy
M   Magenta
P   Hot Pink
AG Apple Green
KG Kelly Green
W   White

1 Square = 1 Inch

Appliquéing the pieces to each block will be easier if you machine-stitch along the traced outline of each appliqué piece, then clip and turn under the ¼-inch allowance. Using the placement marks on the block, position each appliqué piece, then pin down and baste to hold it in place while you slip-stitch. See pages 64-65 for complete appliqué instructions. Continue making all blocks until completed. Finish the reverse appliqué designs as explained on page 70, if you decide to use that technique.

With embroidery floss to match the bodies, embroider the antennae on each butterfly using an outline stitch. Use a running stitch to embroider the flight patterns on those blocks where indicated.

When blocks are finished, pin the patterns to each and trim on the cutting line to ensure that the blocks are accurately sized and perfectly square.

Arrange completed blocks on the floor, using the diagram on page 72 for placement. Sew all blocks together on the sewing machine, using ½-inch seam allowances. Press each seam flat as you sew it. Don't press the seams open, but press them all in the same direction. Continue until all blocks are sewed together to form the quilt top.

Baste together the top, backing, and batting to prepare for the quilting. First place the backing on the floor with open seams up and stretch taut by taping the corners to the floor. Place tape around all edges so the fabric is stretched flat. Unroll the batting and center it on top of the backing. Place the top, right side up, over the batting, centering it as much as possible, and leaving equal portions of the backing fabric showing all around. Make sure all three layers are smooth and flat.

With a long length of quilting thread, start at the center of the quilt and baste diagonally out to each corner, keeping the quilt "sandwich" as flat as possible. Baste horizontally and vertically in the same way. Remove the tape from around the edges of your quilt.

You are now ready to quilt by whichever means you choose. See pages 48-53 for complete instructions on quilting with a floor-standing frame, a quilting hoop, or by the lap method. Machine-quilt if you choose. You'll find those instructions given, too.

Quilt around each appliqué shape and around the edges of each block.

When the quilting is completed, lay the quilt flat and trim the batting to 1½ inches from the edge of the quilt top. Trim the green backing to 2½ inches from the edge of the quilt top.

Fold the backing edge over to the top of the quilt, turning under ½ inch. Pin or baste all the way around so the quilt is bound by the backing. You will have a 1-inch-wide border all around the quilt. On page 52, you'll find complete instructions for forming a binding of the backing fabric and mitering the corners for a finished look.

Machine-stitch the border or slip-stitch by hand.

If you would like to make this quilt for any bed larger than a twin-size, there are several ways of enlarging the design. Here's how to go about it:

For a slight increase in size, simply increase the length and width of the batting sheet to the desired size and increase the length and width of the backing sheet by twice the number of inches you want to add. For example, to change our 67x92-inch design to a 70x95-inch quilt, cut the batting exactly to size, piecing if necessary, and piece the backing to measure 73x98. When the backing is folded over, this will give you a full 4-inch wide border on all sides instead of the 1-inch border shown in our quilt.

The size of the quilt can also be increased by adding narrow strips of apple green fabric between the squares to match the quilt's backing and border. Cut long strips of green 2 inches wide and sew them between all blocks, using ½-inch seams. The only exception is between blocks 14 and 15, which should be sewn together to make a single rectangular block. This procedure will add 3 inches to the width and 4 inches to the length of the quilt. For a greater increase, make the strips wider.

If you want to make a substantial increase in the size of the quilt, you'll have to take other measures. One possibility is to duplicate either side strip of five blocks on the opposite side of the quilt. For example, you could repeat blocks 1, 5, 8, 13, and 18 on the right-hand side of the quilt, or repeat blocks 4, 11, 12, 17, and 21 on the left-hand side of the quilt.

To lengthen the quilt, repeat the bottom row of blocks (18, 19, 20, and 21) at the top. If you choose to enlarge the quilt this way, remember to enlarge the backing and batting accordingly, and to purchase additional fabric for the extra squares.

By repeating the top and bottom or side rows of blocks, you can customize your quilt to whatever bed size you want.

For a king-size bed, you may want to double the entire quilt and make two of each block. Sew the blocks together following the diagram on page 72, then sew the two separate quilt tops together. Simply double the fabric requirements to make a king-size quilt.

Contemporary Grandmother's Flower Garden Quilt

Traditionally, the Grand-mother's Flower Garden quilt is a patchwork project that requires lots of intricate piecing. This contemporary version is done in sewing machine appliqué, allowing you to "grow" your quilt a whole flower at a time, instead of petal by petal. Flamboyant flowers in three different sizes and a startling variety of textures and fabrics combine in a striking way, making this quilt ideal for modern decorating. Remember, though, that a quilt combining fabrics of varying fiber content–such as double knits, cottons, and satins–should be dry-cleaned to keep it in the best condition.

Materials

8 yards muslin
8 yards of print or
  solid color backing
  fabric 45 inches wide
Assorted print fabric
  for flowers and
  centers
1½ yards print fabric
  for borders
Polyester batting

Directions

To make your own version of this quilt, first piece the muslin to the desired size for your bed, lay it on the floor, and place a single layer of quilt batting on top of it.

Next, using the patterns below, cut out as many of each of the three sizes of flowers as are necessary to cover the quilt top, starting at one corner and overlapping blossoms. Vary the sizes, colors, textures, and patterns of the flowers as much as possible. Do not add seam allowances to pattern pieces. Cut contrasting circles for each flower, center them on the flowers and pin in place. Baste all pieces in place through muslin and batting.

Using a ¼-inch satin stitch, machine-appliqué each flower and center in place, stitching through the fabric, batting, and muslin backing. See page 65 for complete instructions on machine appliquéing.

When the quilt top is finished, piece the print fabric to make a backing sheet as large as the quilt. Next cut and piece a 2½-inch-wide strip of binding fabric to go all around the quilt. Fold it in half lengthwise and press. Sew it to the quilt top, right sides together, using a ¼-inch seam allowance. Lay the quilt top on the floor face side down; place the backing fabric on top of it, right side up; turn the binding over the backing; and slip-stitch in place. For a thicker quilt, add extra layers of batting between the muslin and backing fabric. Tack backing fabric to quilt top at 12-inch intervals to keep it from shifting.

1 Square = 1 Inch

Appliquéd and Embroidered Wildflower Coverlet

The eight simple wildflower designs pictured on the opposite page can be artfully combined in any size quilt you desire to make. Our directions are for the quilt shown— a 40x52-inch crib-size coverlet. Each of the floral motifs in the quilt is hand appliquéd and given added emphasis by touches of hand embroidery. By enlarging any of these designs, you can use them in lots of different projects—as our machine appliquéd pillow illustrates.

Materials

2¾ yards white
  45-inch cotton blend
  fabric
1½ yards green
  45-inch fabric
Scraps of fabric in colors
  for flowers
Pearl cotton embroidery thread
Polyester batting

Directions

To make this wildflower coverlet, cut 12 11-inch square blocks of white fabric. Next enlarge the designs shown on pages 82-83. Make a properly sized pattern on tracing paper, then use it to make cutting patterns for each appliqué piece. With carbon paper, trace the appliqué shapes from the tracing paper to heavy paper or lightweight cardboard. Keep the tracing paper pattern intact to use as a placement guide.

Use the photo opposite as a color guide, and cut appliqué pieces of the fabric colors shown. Add ¼-inch seam allowances to each appliqué shape, and work one block at a time. Follow the instructions on pages 64-65 for hand appliquéing. When the appliqué pieces have been hand-stitched in place, embroider leaves, stems, and details on each flower as indicated on the pattern. For our 12-block quilt, three of the eight flower patterns are repeated twice, and we included a personal block with embroidered name and birthdate in the lower right-hand corner.

When all blocks have been appliquéd and embroidered, press them gently to remove all wrinkles. Make a 10½-inch square of cardboard and place on the appliquéd block. Be sure the flower is positioned the way you want it, then mark around the cardboard square and trim excess fabric away so you have a 10½-inch square block. Finished quilt blocks are 10 inches. Sew with ¼-inch seam allowances.

Cut nine green strips 2½x10½ inches. Lay appliquéd blocks on the floor in the desired arrangement. Using ¼-inch seam allowances, sew together four blocks with three green strips between. Strips should be sewn between the top of one block and the bottom of the next. Make three vertical rows of blocks. Cut two strips of green fabric 2½x46½ inches. Using ¼-inch seam allowances, sew these two strips between the three rows of blocks to form the completed block section of the quilt.

Cut the border strips of green fabric. You'll need two strips 3½x46½ inches, two strips 3½x34½ inches, and four squares 3½x3½ inches.

Sew the two 46½-inch-long strips to the outside side edges of the block section. Next sew a 3½-inch square at each end of the two 3½ x 34½-inch strips. Pin these two pieced strips at the top and bottom of the block section. Make sure the seams match so the small corner square lines up with the border strip that joins it. Sew with a ¼-inch seam allowance.

Press all seams away from the white blocks and toward the green strips that surround them. Following the instructions beginning on page 46, assemble the completed quilt top, batting, and backing. Cut the backing from the remainder of the white fabric. Machine or hand quilt along the seam lines of the blocks and green strips. Finish the edges as desired.

To make a companion pillow, as shown, enlarge a single flower block to any size you choose—from 12 to 18 inches. Machine-appliqué the pillow top using techniques outlined in general appliqué instructions (pages 64-65). Make or buy covered cording to edge the pillow. Sew the cording to the finished pillow top with the raw edges of the cording placed along the raw edges of the right side of the pillow. Cut the pillow back to the appropriate size and sew to the front, right sides together. Leave one side open, turn, and insert pillow form. Stitch closed.

continued

Appliquéd and Embroidered Wildflower Coverlet *(continued)*

Clover

Violet

Bachelor Button

Hepatica

Dandelion

Gilia

California Poppy

Black Eyed Susan

FOR CATHERINE
2-14-1976

1 Square = 1 Inch

EMBROIDERY STITCH GUIDE

1 Satin Stitch
2 Outline Stitch
3 Running Stitch
4 French Knot

Appliquéd and Quilted Window Wall Hanging

For a room without a view, create one . . . with soft fabric fields and enchanting calico mountains.

Materials
Medium brown fabric for quilt background and bias binding
Fabric scraps for appliqué
Polyester batting

Directions
Enlarge the drawing below and trace onto the brown background fabric. Cut out all appliqué pieces in your choice of fabrics, adding seam allowances.

Baste and press under the seam allowance on each piece. Position the appliqué pieces according to the diagram, and stitch in place (see pages 64-65).

Make slits in the background fabric behind each appliquéd area, lightly stuff with batting, then whipstitch openings closed. Assemble according to directions on page 46. Quilt as desired and finish edges with bias binding.

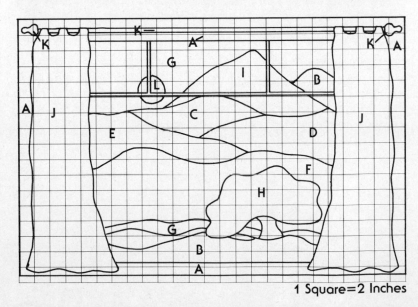

1 Square = 2 Inches

COLOR KEY

A Medium Brown
B Black
C Green Print
D Polka Dot
E Medium Green
F Dark Green
G Blue
H Light Green
I Beige
J Floral Print
K Brass
L Sun Yellow

Patchwork Plus—

Novelty Projects

Before anyone starts to think that the world of patchwork takes itself too seriously, we'd like to show you the lighter side of the craft. In this section, we feature novelty projects that take patchwork, quilting, and appliqué out of their traditional roles and give them a chance to have a little fun. You'll see appliqué for the bedroom, but this time as a headboard, not a quilt. There are some projects any youngster would love—including an exercise mat and a big fat red hen nesting on a quilt. Complete diagrams and instructions are given for a veritable album of quilting. And, on the next pages, you'll learn how to turn the kids loose with a box of fabric crayons to create the fun-loving quilt shown here. With a little imagination, there's no telling what you can do with patchwork, quilting, and appliqué.

A Child-Art Crayon Quilt

A crayon quilt can keep the whole family busy. On sheets of drawing paper, measure 12-inch squares and outline them lightly in pencil. Quilt artists should confine their drawings to this area, since the pencil lines represent the quilt block seams and anything beyond these lines will be lost on the finished squares.

Materials

1 set of Crayola brand
  fabric crayons
Medium-weight drawing
  paper
17 13-inch squares of
  white, synthetic fabric
18 13-inch squares of
  bright color fabric
2¾ yards border fabric
1 sheet or 6 yards of
  backing fabric
Polyester quilt batting

Directions

Before starting work on your quilt drawings, make a color test to see how well the fabric you've selected will take the crayon dye. This test will also show your artists how the colors will look when transferred to fabric. You'll find colors appear much more intense on fabric than on drawing paper. To make the color test, simply fill in small squares of each color on drawing paper and transfer the "test sheet" to a left-over piece of the fabric to be used for the quilt squares.

In planning designs for the quilt, keep in mind that drawings will transfer backwards. In the case of drawings with written captions, write the caption on a separate piece of paper, then trace it in reverse with crayon onto the main design.

To transfer crayon drawings to quilt squares, follow crayon package directions. Start by placing on the ironing board several folded sheets of newspaper, topped with a sheet of clean white paper. Place a square of white fabric on top of this ironing "pad." Using a stiff-bristled brush, brush all stray specks of crayon wax off the design paper before you place it on the fabric so they won't transfer. Lay the clean crayon design face down on the fabric, making sure the design is centered on the square. Finally, place another clean sheet of white paper between the transfer and the iron to avoid soiling the iron.

Turn the iron to the cotton setting to provide enough heat for transferring the crayon design effectively. Press with a steady, strong pressure over the entire design until the color becomes slightly visible through the top sheet of paper. Check frequently by carefully lifting a corner of the design to make sure the fabric is not scorching and the color is transferring evenly. Be careful not to shift the drawing on the fabric or you will blur the color and outline on the print. Once transferred to synthetic fabric, the crayon colors are permanent and completely washable. When transferred to all-cotton fabric, the crayon colors are softer and less color-fast.

To assemble the quilt, arrange the quilt blocks in seven rows of five squares each, alternating solid color and crayon squares. Arrange quilt so that four strips start and end with solid color blocks, and three strips start and end with crayon blocks. Join blocks into strips and then join strips into the completed quilt top, using ½-inch seam allowances. Press all seams toward solid color blocks.

Lay quilt backing out on the floor, wrong side up. Lay quilt batting on top of backing, followed by the quilt front, face up. Follow instructions given on page 49 for pinning and basting all layers together, then machine-stitch along all vertical and horizontal seam lines. Bind the quilt with seven-inch-wide strips of solid color fabric, folded in half lengthwise over three-inch-wide strips of batting to give a soft, puffy edging. To attach the binding, stitch the fabric strip to the top-side of the quilt, right sides together. Miter corners and turn the edging to the back of the quilt. Blindstitch the edging in place. The finished quilt measures approximately 66x90 inches.

It's easy to make a crayon quilt to fit any size bed by simply changing the total number of 12-inch finished squares used. A twin-size quilt (54x90 inches) would require 14 solid color squares and 14 crayon squares arranged four squares wide and seven squares long. For a queen-size quilt (78x102 inches), use 24 squares of each (solid color and crayon) arranged six squares wide by eight squares long. A king-size quilt (90x102 inches) requires 28 squares of each type arranged seven squares wide and eight squares long.

With a little family cooperation, you can design and stitch a colorful crayon quilt in no time at all. While the youngsters are busy creating the art (above, left), Mom transfers their finished drawings onto fabric squares using a hot iron. The pictures must be pressed with strong, steady pressure to transfer completely (bottom, left). Crayon squares reproduced on synthetic fabrics are more brilliant and less likely to fade than on all-cotton material (above).

Appliquéd Headboard

Appliqué goes to the head of the bed with this classic, padded satin headboard. Our flowering vine design is worked in soft shades of green and dusty rose, but this delicate, stylized look can be adapted to whatever color scheme complements your bedroom.

Materials

1½ yards of 54-inch-wide eggshell satin (for twin-size headboard)
Scraps of satin in dark green, light green, dusty rose, and light pink
1 quilt bat
¼-inch plywood
3 yards muslin or inexpensive backing fabric
Staple gun or tacks
Fusible webbing

Directions

Start by enlarging the pattern below. Using the outline of the headboard pattern as a general guide, cut a piece of ¼-inch plywood that's 43 inches wide and 36 inches high at the peak of the headboard. Slope the contour of the top to conform to the pattern. These measurements are for a single or twin-size bed. To adapt the headboard to a full- or oversize bed, enlarge the drawing accordingly.

When the drawing is enlarged to the desired size, cut patterns for the flower, leaves, and stems using lightweight cardboard. Place each cardboard template on the wrong side of the appropriate color satin fabric, trace around edges, and cut out; do *not* add seam allowances. (Color key for diagram: D = dark green, L = light green, R = dusty rose, P = pink, E = eggshell.) Once the flowering vine and pink border strips are cut, arrange them in the proper place on the eggshell satin beginning nine inches from the top edge and six inches from each outer edge. Excess fabric will be folded and stapled to the plywood backing.

Cut pieces of fusible webbing using your cardboard templates as guides. Position the cut webbing under each satin piece and fuse them to the eggshell satin background fabric with a steam iron. Be sure that no webbing shows outside the edges of the satin. Fusing the appliqué pieces to the satin background fabric keeps them from slipping as you sew them in place. Cut and add border strips last.

Cut a piece of muslin and quilt batting that are the same dimensions as the eggshell satin. Sandwich the batting between the muslin backing and the satin, and baste all three layers together. Machine-appliqué around each fused design using ¼-inch satin stitch. Work slowly and carefully so that the stitching goes through all three layers. Hand-embroider the center of the flower in pink satin stitch.

Once the design is appliquéd, position the eggshell satin front on the plywood headboard. Smooth out the satin, turning the excess fabric to the back of the plywood, and staple or tack the fabric in place. Trim off the excess satin close to the staples.

To conceal the raw edges, cut a piece of backing fabric to fit the plywood headboard. Turn under the edges one inch and machine-hem. Place the backing against the plywood, then whipstitch it to the satin.

To adapt this project to a rectangular padded headboard, enlarge the design and turn it upside down so the straight edge is at the top. Then customize the border to conform to this rectangular shape.

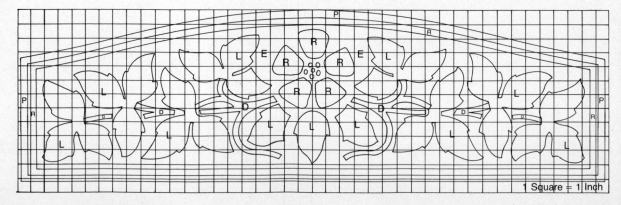

1 Square = 1 Inch

Red Hen Appliquéd Quilt

The Little Red Hen of storybook fame has gone supersize on this zany children's quilt. And any youngster will welcome this bright addition to his or her bedroom. Once the 41x65-inch coverlet is quilted, simply enlarge the pattern pieces, cut out the shapes, and stitch them onto the background.

Materials

2 yards 45-inch-wide red-orange fabric for backing
2 yards 45-inch-wide white fabric
1 yard red-orange washable velveteen for chicken
Yellow-orange and white fabric scraps
Blanket binding
Polyester quilt batting

1 Square = 5 Inches

Directions

To make this chunky chicken quilt first layer red-orange backing fabric, batting, and white top fabric. Starting one inch from the edges, mark the quilt top at 6-inch intervals along the top and bottom edges, and in 7-inch intervals along the sides. Stitch horizontal and vertical lines with black thread to create a quilted chicken wire background.

Enlarge the chicken pattern at left and cut from velveteen fabric. Pin the hen to a piece of quilt batting and baste the two layers together. Trim the batting to the fabric edge. Cut the eyes from white fabric. Hand-baste the eyes in place, then outline with satin zigzag stitch. Follow the same procedure with the beak. Stitch pupils and nostrils in black satin zigzag stitch. Position the chicken on the quilt, pin and baste in place, then satin-stitch on the machine. Zigzag yellow straws at the base of the chick. Cut two eggs from white fabric, turn under ¼ inch, and hand-stitch to the quilt, stuffing with batting as you stitch. Attach blanket binding.

Patchwork Exercise Mat

This wall-hung exercise mat will be a hit with your junior gymnasts because it also doubles as a cozy nap mat for quieter times. This one features six abstract patchwork acrobats made of assorted fabric squares and triangles.

Materials

4 yards red print fabric (#1)
1½ yards navy fabric (#2)
1 yard navy and red print fabric (#3)
1½ yards blue and white check fabric (#4)
½ yard navy and white print fabric (#5)
½ yard orange print fabric (#6)
¼ yard orange gingham (#7)
Scraps of red and black polka dot fabric
Polyester quilt batting
4 plastic drapery rings

Directions

Enlarge the drawing at the right to full-size and use it as a placement guide. Each 16-inch square acrobat block is pieced entirely of squares and triangles; heads are appliquéd on last. Following diagram, cut several square and triangular templates and add ¼-inch seam allowances to all pieces. Cut out and piece blocks following diagram at right. Do not add heads. Begin by cutting #1 backing fabric and batting to 44½x60½ inches. Cut two 4½x36½-inch and two 4½x60½-inch pieces for the border.

Stitch together completed acrobat blocks. Press seams open. Cut two 2½x32½-inch and two 2½x52½-inch pieces from fabric #2. Sew strips to block section and border pieces to outside edges. Cut head sections, turn under ¼ inch and appliqué in place. Place finished patchwork over batting, right side up. Lay backing over patchwork, right side down. Stitch around all four sides, leaving opening for turning. Turn, and stitch closed. Add rings for hanging.

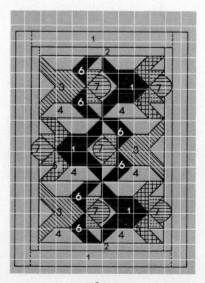

1 Square = 4 Inches

A Quilter's Quilt

If, in the course of this book, you've come to love quilts and quilting, then here's a project made to order for you. In this one quilt you'll be able to use all the techniques you've learned and in a most imaginative way. What is a quilt? In this case it's a spectacular 15-block storybook of quilting.

Materials

2 yards 45-inch blue fabric
   for borders
Fifteen 12-inch squares of
   fabric for block
   backgrounds
Assorted scraps of print
   and colored fabrics
Iron-on bonding fabric
White fabric paint
White sheet for backing
Polyester batting

Directions

To make this 48x76-inch quilt, collect all needed materials and enlarge the designs on the following pages (94-95). Make two copies of each block on tracing paper. You'll need one to cut into individual pattern pieces and one to lay over each block as a placement guide when you appliqué.

Press background fabrics smooth and cut out 12-inch-square blocks. Though blocks are finished to 10 inches, they're cut large to allow for take-up of fabric during the appliqué process. If a block is composed of several background pieces, machine-sew all pieces together and press the seams to one side.

Cut the larger appliqué pieces by laying the tracing paper pattern on the right side of the fabric and adding ¼-inch seam allowances to all edges. To simplify appliquéing the letters and small pieces, use iron-on bonding fabric. Draw exactly around the edge of pattern pieces on the shiny (bonding) surface of the iron-on fabric. Cut the pieces out and bond to the back of the print fabric to be appliquéd. Then cut the piece out of the print, adding ¼-inch seam allowance. To appliqué, turn under the seam allowance and slip-stitch each piece to the background. When appliquéing, refer to the photo of our quilt, since some pieces are behind others and must be sewn on first. As you pin and sew on each piece, lay the tracing paper pattern of the whole block over the work to check the placement of the pieces. Appliqué all blocks before quilting.

Each block is made up of different design elements and needlework techniques. Some require special treatment, so study each square carefully as you work. Here are some tips that may help with the individual blocks:

The *Color* block features a fabric rainbow. You need not stitch down the bottom edge of each strip because the next one overlaps it. Stitch down the bottom of only the yellow strip. Add the letters and hand, and embroider the hand details.

On the *Love* block, the "L" and "V" are one applique piece. The "E" and heart are separate.

The *Soft/Snoozy* square actually contains a block within a block. Appliqué the "Z's" on a separate piece of fabric, then appliqué that fabric to the main block. Appliqué sheep's heads, bodies, then ears. Eyes and legs are embroidered in simple outline stitch.

The *Patchwork* block should be treated as two pieces. Add the letters to red fabric, then add a piece composed of two rows of patchwork squares. Appliqué the patchwork cat to a rectangle of red fabric, and embroider the details. Stitch that block to the lower right corner of the patchwork on the main block.

To work the *Appliquéd* block, stitch on design elements in the following order: basket handle, basket, flowers, then the letters (the basket texture will be quilted later).

The *Warm* block is worked in this sequence: Appliqué the sun and rings by themselves, then pin onto the background. Slip points of the sun behind outer ring and stitch points down. Now stitch the sun and rings down. Attach letters to the hill, and appliqué hill overlapping the sun. Add flowers and embroider stems and sun.

For the *Gentle Hands* block, appliqué the blue skirt, bodice, quilt, arms, hands, collar, face, hair, and glasses in that order. Add letters and embroidery.

continued

WHAT IS A QUILT? A QUILT IS....

EMBROIDERED DESIGNS THAT MAKE THE QUILT GAY
ARE PLEASURES AND DUTIES WE FIND ON OUR WAY
HOPE, LOVE AND KISSES ARE STITCHES SO BRIGHT
WHICH DECORATE LIFE WITH GLEAMS OF DELIGHT
WHILE SYMPATHY SWEET IS THE LINING TO HOLD
THE ODD SCRAPS OF FATE WHICH WE CANNOT CONTROL
WE ARE BETTER THAN PATCHWORK BECAUSE OF THE SOUL.

...FOUND
EMBROIDERED
ON BACK OF
1890 QUILT.

A Quilter's Quilt (continued)

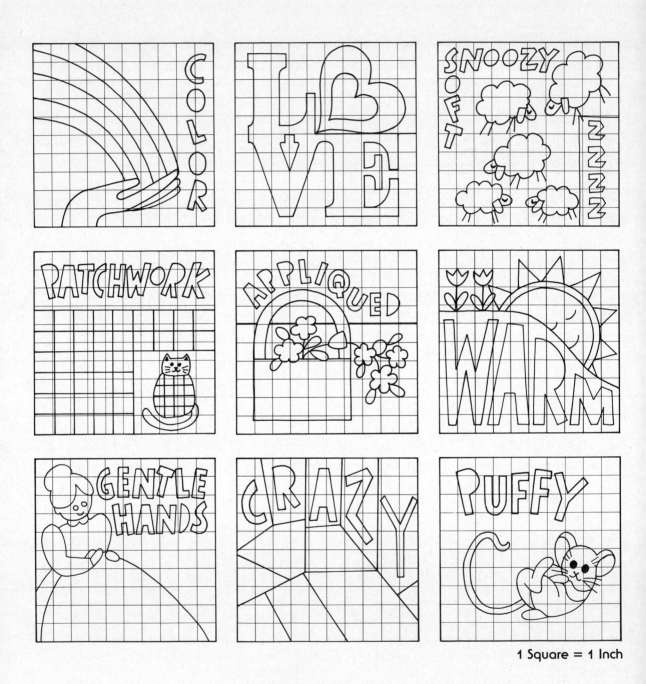

1 Square = 1 Inch

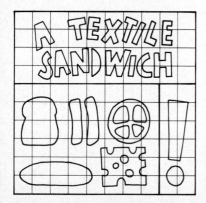

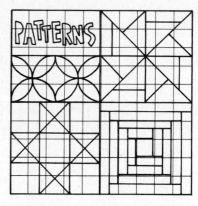

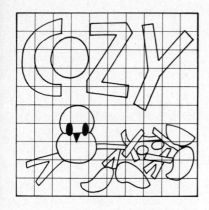

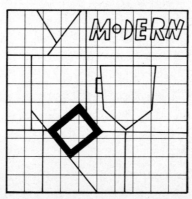

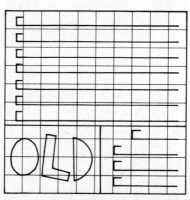

1 Square = 1 Inch

EMBROIDERED DESIGNS THAT MAKE THE QUILT GAY
ARE PLEASURES AND DUTIES WE FIND ON OUR WAY
HOPE, LOVE AND KISSES ARE STITCHES SO BRIGHT
WHICH DECORATE LIFE WITH GLEAMS OF DELIGHT
WHILE SYMPATHY SWEET IS THE LINING TO HOLD
THE ODD SCRAPS OF FATE WHICH WE CANNOT CONTROL
WE ARE BETTER THAN PATCHWORK BECAUSE OF THE SOUL.

FOUND EMBROIDERED ON BACK OF 1890 QUILT.

continued

A Quilter's Quilt *(continued)*

The *Crazy* quilt block is pieced on the sewing machine. Add letters. The zigzag edging on the pieces is added at the time of quilting.

The *Puffy* block is appliquéd with the letters, mouse, ears and tail. Embroider details. Tie this block; don't quilt it.

The *Cozy* square is easier if you piece the bird and leaves on the machine before you cut them out. Appliqué pieces in this order: nest, branches, leaves, eggs, bird, and letters. Embroider details.

Appliqué *A Good Nite* block. Add cheek last. Embroider eye and smile.

The *Patterns* block is treated as four separate pieces. Make the first piece and appliqué the letters. Make "Cathedral Window" rectangle, then attach to the letters block. Do sections in "Pinwheel," "Star," and "Log Cabin" designs. Join all sections together.

To make *A Textile Sandwich*, appliqué the letters to red fabric; the exclamation point to green, pieced to pink. Appliqué sandwich "fixin's," add embroidery details, and join the two pieces together.

The *Modern* square is treated as three strips. Appliqué letters and piece the rest of the top horizontal strip. Piece the center strip, attaching the pocket with machine-stitching outline. Piece the bottom strip, then join all three and appliqué the off-center red square onto the block.

To print the letters on the *Old* square, first print the poem in block letters on tracing paper. Lay carbon paper and the pattern on the fabric and tape the corners down. Trace over letters carefully with a dry ballpoint. Remove carbon and pattern and paint letters with fabric paint, laying on the paint in even strokes. When dry, paint a second coat. After that coat has dried, join the appliquéd lettered piece and the two painted pieces to form the complete block.

To complete quilt, layer 12-inch squares of sheet and polyester batting under each block. Baste all layers together. Machine quilt according to instructions given on page 50, using about eight stitches to the inch. Use white thread in the bobbin and change the top thread to match the face fabric. Stitch around all letters and designs, making sure no area larger than three or four inches is left unquilted.

Cut a 10-inch square of cardboard, lay it on the quilted blocks, and trace around, leaving a ¼-inch seam allowance. Stitch edges carefully, then trim off excess fabric.

Cut the following panels from both the blue fabric and sheet backing (these measurements include a ½-inch seam allowance): Ten panels 5x11 inches to use between three block groups across the quilt; four panels 5x39 inches to use between the five rows of blocks vertically; two panels 6x67 inches for the two long sides of the quilt; and two panels 6x49 inches for the top and bottom edges. Cut matching batting pieces and baste to front fabric.

Make five strips of three blocks each, then join these five strips with the four panels to form the body of the quilt. Machine-sew both front panel edges. Machine-sew one backing panel edge, then hand-sew the other one in place. Add the side panels, leaving the outside edges open. Appliqué letters to the top strip, then add the top and bottom strips to the quilt. To finish the quilt, turn the front panel edges back over the backing and slip-stitch the face fabric to the backing.

We are happy to acknowledge our indebtedness and express our sincere thanks to the following people for their valuable help in producing this book.

Designers

Janet DeBard 11
Joan Cravens 12
Ciba Vaughan 14-15, 36-37, 84-85
Ginny Lee Snow 17
John Stith 19
Vicki Olivo 20-21
Michael Gold 26-37
Mrs. Arthur Woodburn .. 38-39
Erma Wink 52-53, 58-59
Myrtl Thomas 54-55
Rosie Fischer 60-61, 62-63, 68-69
Charlotte Patera 70-77
Mimi Shimmin 80-81
Ocean Beach Quilters ... 80-81, 83
Diana Messerly 88-89
Molli Nickell 90
Jan Bowman 92-96

Acknowledgments

Quilts and Other Comforts
   Denver, Colorado 4-5
Quilts in the Attic
   Denver, Colorado 4-5
Rainbow Shop
   Beverly Hills,
   California 78-79
Distlefink
   New York, New York 91
Mrs. Wigg's Cabbage Patch, Inc.
   Des Moines, Iowa
Norma Buferd
Patricia Cooper
Jean LemMon